ASSEMBLE THE TRIBE

ASSEMBLE THE

tribe

Believe in Your Value.
Find Belonging. Be Different.

LEAH J M DEAN

HOUNDSTOOTH
PRESS

Cover photo: Kayla McConnie of @her.storyartistry
Makeup: Oneeka Williams
Book Coach: Arlene Gale, Book Writing Business Coach for assistance with organizing and facilitating the writing process. BookWritingBusiness.com

The personal stories in this book are based on the experiences of the author and have been constructed for illustrative purposes only. Unless specifically requested, all of the names of the individuals in this book have been changed. Where individuals may be identifiable, they have granted permission to the author and the publisher to use their stories and/or facts about their lives.

ASSEMBLE THE TRIBE
Believe in Your Value. Find Belonging. Be Different.

ISBN   978-1-5445-1581-6 *Hardcover*
       978-1-5445-1580-9 *Paperback*
       978-1-5445-1579-3 *Ebook*
       978-1-5445-1582-3 *Audiobook*

To Taylor and the next generation of women:

May your world be a different place.

A place where you can find your Tribes

and never be alone.

With all my love,

Mom

CONTENTS

ACKNOWLEDGMENTS

I never intended to write a book. It wasn't on my radar until one night, I woke up with a start, and the outline for the book poured onto the pages as I typed—it literally wrote itself. As a result, I believe *Assemble the Tribe* is divinely inspired. I thank God for entrusting me with this message, and I hope to share it in a way that honors the gift.

The process of writing a book is in many ways like birthing a baby. You carry it for months, nurture it inside of you, and then give birth to the baby whom you hope will be loved by everyone he or she meets. While you can never know for sure, you also have hope that your baby will change the world for good. Birthing a baby also requires support. In order to bring the baby into the world, you rely on the help and wisdom of experts, family, and friends. This project is no different, and I am grateful to everyone who has contributed to my journey.

My book-writing coach and editor, Arlene Gale. At so many points in the process, you were the wind beneath my wings. When I wondered if I was on the right track, your encouragement, enthusiasm, passion, and shared belief about the power of mindset made us the perfect team. Thank you, thank you, thank you.

The entire Tribe at Scribe Publishing. You have been an amazing partner from day one. From the contracting phase to the moment I unpackaged my first book, it has been a pleasure to work with you to bring this project to life. Thank you!

My Tribe, my amazing Tribe, male and female, you know who you are, too many to name. What an amazing gift you have been to me at each step in the process. Thank you for the calls, check-ins, encouragement, and stories. Thank you for helping me to think things through and develop concepts, and some days just giving me the space to talk. I can't imagine what the journey would be like without you cheering me on along the way.

A special thanks to Dr. Kelly Holder, Dr. Meira Epplein, Staci Danford, and Ann Dorgan for lending your wisdom and expertise to the project. I also want to thank Charlee Ashkettle, Chanel Bean, Ivona and Bria Bernard, Ingrid Botelho, Celia Brown, Cammy Burrows, Shevy Easton, Andrea DeSouza, Antonia Holder, Maria Holder, Sheila Holder, Amy Kurland, Dana Lightbourne, Simona-Mills Pitcher, Patrina O'Conner-Paynter, Amanda Morgan, Michelle Proctor, Tiffany Richardson, Kim Rinker, Kay Trott, Jane Smith, Jennifer Wales, and my mom, Julie Richardson, for your contributions, editing, and support to help get the book over the finish line.

Real Queens, I seriously could not have done this without you. Thank you for allowing me to travel life's journey with you for nearly twenty years. I have learned so much from our time together, and you are a big part of my inspiration for this book.

Thank you for showing me that, as women, we can fix each other's crowns, have each other's backs, and live our best lives.

Mom, Dad, Ralph and Tiffany, Brenton and Tasha, Tesa, and my nieces and nephews: Nina, Noelle, Ryla, Raya, Eli, Zakari, Uriah, Xavier, and Gia. Thank you for your love and support. I could not ask for a more caring group of cheerleaders than my family. True Tribe begins at home; thank you for teaching me what that means.

Tristan, thank you for supporting me in this process. Thank you for listening to my stories and sharing your opinions. You continue to amaze me. You are wise beyond your years. I hope the concepts in this book will be of value and help you understand women just a bit better!

Taylor, you have been my biggest fan from the very start. You and the Young Original Unstoppable girls were my inspiration to finish this book so future generations of young women can find their Tribes and never feel alone. Thank you for your love and generational wisdom.

My husband, Terrance. I am who I am, a better version of me, because of you. For more than twenty years, you have supported my MANY exploits and have helped me to understand what it means to *Believe + Belong and Be Different*. Thank you for your patience, suggestions, tech support, and understanding. You are amazing.

INTRODUCTION

My story of Tribe began when I was about eight years old. I am 100 percent sure I was not cognizant that I was searching for a Tribe at the time. However, as I look back, it seems my entire life has been a journey toward my passion for helping people to *Assemble the Tribe.*

Maybe it was my observations about the women around me. Maybe it was the middle school experience when groups of girls didn't get along. The fact remained firmly implanted in my mind: I was better off without a lot of females in my life. Now don't get me wrong—I had many positive female friends over the years, many of whom are very active in my life today. However, as a tween, teen, college student, and young professional, even though I subconsciously wanted these connections, I was afraid of the idea of lots of female interactions.

Even childhood movies and books sent me mixed messages. Some books focused on what is achieved when friends come together, while other stories and fairy tales highlighted the reality of how complicated, full of drama, and unkind women and girls can be.

Rather than complicate my life at that time, I decided to do what many teenage girls do: hang out with the guys. With two brothers, some days hanging with the guys was my only choice, and frankly it was easy. Most days all I had to do was play cricket or kick a soccer ball around, enjoy myself, and laugh.

This self-imposed anti-girl strategy was brilliant during elementary school, but as a teen and college student, my male friendships became more complicated. This was especially true when my childhood "male best friends" started to date. I found out the hard way that having me as a female best friend was not a winning boyfriend strategy for them and the girls they were dating.

Thankfully my college years were busy. I didn't have time to feel distressed about these changes to my friend circle. This continued into the early stages of my career, when something happened to change my life forever.

THE DATA IS IN

Over the years, as I coached women and mentored up-and-coming professionals, I heard parts of my story repeated over and over again:

"Female relationships are just too much work."

"Women are complicated."

"Young girls are difficult and catty."

"It's difficult to trust women, especially groups of women."

And my favorite: "I prefer to just hang out with the guys."

I have heard women describe, with deep pain, the desire to connect and find a sense of belonging, yet struggle to take the next step and move toward relationship. I traveled the world, attending women's conferences. Over the years, I have also produced events for women and girls. In the process I discovered, whether it's twenty or ten thousand women in a room, we can create meaningful connections together.

Wanting to understand the dynamics of female relationships on a deeper level, I decided to conduct a study. I surveyed 1,269 women across Bermuda, the United States, and Canada. The primary goal was to understand the perspective of the female group more deeply.

The data is in and it shows, for example, 54 percent of women surveyed have no philosophy about female groups. Of the 46 percent of women who do have a philosophy about female groups, nearly half don't trust women or believe female groups are too much work.

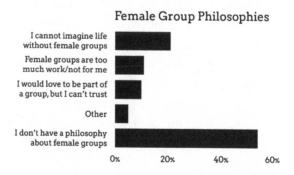

Female Group Philosophies

While I was hoping for a different result, the data supports that female relationships can be hard. My hope, my goal, is that *Assemble the Tribe* will uncomplicate the complicated and help us to thrive in our relationships.

WHO SHOULD READ THIS BOOK

I want to be up front: *Assemble the Tribe* was explicitly written with women and female connections in mind. As women, our issues are unique, and it's time to have a conversation about how female relationships impact our lives and can change the world.

Are you looking for female friendships and connections, but they have eluded you?

Were you hurt and then abandoned all hope of making meaningful long-term female connections?

Are you one of those women who never considered or thought about the concept of Tribe?

Do you believe in the value of Tribe and perhaps want to go deeper?

Perhaps you have a role in raising the next generation of girls as a parent, grandparent, aunt, uncle, teacher, or coach, and want to be a better guide to these girls. Read this book. Helping girls and young women navigate the complexities of life may leave you feeling ill-equipped. This book is for you, too.

No matter where you are on your journey, *Assemble the Tribe* has something for women of all ages and their supporters.

WHAT TO EXPECT FROM THIS BOOK

Assemble the Tribe is a call to action to live our best lives and change the world through life-changing female relationships. This book has four core sections:

PART 1: WHY TRIBES MATTER

Many of us, at some point in our lives, have questioned if tionship or friendship is worth it. This first section of *Assemble the Tribe* lays the foundation for why finding and thriving with our Tribes is not optional. Chapter 1 defines what a Tribe is and what it means to have a Tribe mindset. I also introduce my Tribe-building formula: Believe + Belong = Be Different, which is the foundation for how we assemble our Tribes. Chapter 2 explores the incredible impact Tribes have on our health, happiness, and life span. Finally, chapter 3 examines historical, scientific, and societal reasons why healthy relationships with women matter.

 PART 2: BELIEVE + BELONG

Sometimes, finding our Tribes can feel overwhelming and complicated. However, it can also be exciting, empowering, and life-changing. Chapters 5 through 8 explore the different levels of Tribe and how to navigate each one effectively. Chapters 9 and 10 are about how to navigate and be open to new relationships when we are busy juggling immediate and extended family, work, and other responsibilities. Finally, we explore what to do when openness and new relationships scare us and how to deal with our fears.

PART 3: BE DIFFERENT (LIVING LIFE WITH YOUR TRIBE)

Now it's time to get hands-on and practical in chapter 12 by exploring a simple process to create healthy Tribes. Chapter 13 examines some of the ways we experience happiness and joy with our Tribes. Then in chapter 14 we take a look at many of the common challenges that inevitably come along with female relationships and how to approach them differently. Chapter

15 explores what to do when we experience rejection, and our relationships are temporarily or permanently broken.

PART 4: BE DIFFERENT (BEYOND THE TRIBE)

In the final section, we wrap up the book by putting it all together and examining how we can leverage our new Tribe mindset. Chapters 17 and 18 explore ways to use the Tribe-building formula to think differently and change how we raise our girls, discover our innate purpose, and have a greater impact on the world.

One of the best ways to connect with a topic is through stories. At the end of each section, there's a story of a woman who is part of my Tribe. These are real women who have struggled and triumphed with embracing a Tribe mindset. Their stories are our stories. Their struggles are our struggles. Their stories remind us that we are not alone and that ultimately, finding our Tribes does matter.

Finally, at the end of each chapter, there is a summary of the chapter's key points and a series of reflection questions. Each chapter concludes with exercises and suggestions to encourage readers to find ways to Be Different. These sections can be completed alone or with a Tribe you are part of or creating.

IT'S TIME TO ASSEMBLE THE TRIBE

While there are a great many movements around the world focusing on bringing people together, the female connection is sometimes elusive. The question is: Is there another way? Are there zones of relationship and friendship where there are:

- Opinions, but no judgments.
- Different personalities, but understanding and tolerance.
- Failings, but assumptions of good intent.
- Imperfection, but acceptance.

Is it possible women can find this place, and maybe, just maybe, change generations of women to come?

Turn the page and prepare to unleash a new way of thinking, a new way of living, a values system, and a mindset that will bring us closer together! Let's *Assemble the Tribe*!

PART 1

Why Tribes Matter

CHAPTER 1

WHAT IS TRIBE?

The journey to finding our Tribes can be complicated. We begin our journey of *Assemble the Tribe* by examining what is Tribe and what it means to have a Tribe mindset.

Defining the core concepts of Tribe is important. Tribes are often associated with "primitive" or "less progressive" ways of living. At other times the word can evoke deep emotions or help develop bonds. In recent history, at its best, the word "Tribe" is used to create movements, and at its worst, to rip relationships apart as people entrench into individual beliefs or political divides. For these reasons, it is important for us to think about Tribes in a universal way to get the most benefit from this book.

While writing *Assemble the Tribe*, I was often asked: "Are you sure, really sure, you want to use that word?"

At times I was not sure if I wanted to wade into the debate. However, the more I researched and wrote, the more I knew that the word "Tribe" for all its flaws and complexities was the right way to navigate this journey.

DEFINING TRIBE

If we delve deeply into the history of the word Tribe, we will discover it goes back to thirteenth-century middle-English literature. Derived from the French word *tribu* and the Latin word *tribus*, the word originally referred to the three ethnic Tribes of Rome. Other early references cite the Twelve Tribes of Israel.

The Merriam-Webster dictionary has four definitions of the word "Tribe," which includes families, clans, groups of people with common interests, and even a classification below a subfamily such as the cat or rose Tribe.[1] Based on these definitions alone, it is clear to see the word can mean many things to different people.

The use of the word "Tribe" has also moved into mainstream popular language. I Googled the word "Tribe" and within seconds got back 931,000,000 results. The findings ranged from ethnic references, to names of companies, sports teams, branding and marketing firms, and groups on Instagram. The word "Tribe" is everywhere.

In the academic realm, the use of the word Tribe is complicated. Some scholars use it, while others say to throw it out. In his book *The Notion of Tribe,* Morton H. Fried, professor of anthropology and notable contributor to the fields of social and political theory, contends, "The term is so ambiguous and confusing that it should be abandoned by social scientists."[2]

Given this word-use complexity, for the purpose of this book, I created a simplified definition of Tribe:

Tribe: Individually complex people with shared beliefs, values, or interests, who choose to come together, in various ways (physical, virtual, informal), to create relationships.

When we consider our Tribes, it is important to remember the compositions of Tribes are different from what most of us think. When most of us envisage Tribes, we think about groups, typically made up of three or more. However, a group is defined as two or more figures forming a complete unit.[3] That means your best buddy, an acquaintance you met at a conference, a running club mate—any one-to-one relationship can be part of your Tribe. Equally, any group of three or more people can be part of your Tribe.

Now that we have defined Tribe, the million-dollar question becomes: how do we thrive in our Tribes? But before we jump in to answer that question, you may recall that in the introduction I said that I did not really think about relationships and Tribes until something happened to change my perspective forever. Here's that story.

LIFE IS SHORT—DON'T WASTE IT

As a young career woman, my experience and perspective had not evolved much when it came to relationships, especially relationships with women. However, on my wedding day, a seed was planted that changed it all.

In a quiet moment waiting to walk down the aisle, I asked my childhood mentor and lady-in-waiting, Alexa, for some words of wisdom. Alexa was barely five feet tall and full of energy. Her beautiful smile and big laugh penetrated your soul. Even with three young kids, her dark hair and clothing were always stylish and impeccable.

When I was around the age of fourteen, Alexa picked me up like a stray. One day after school, I was at my dad's office waiting for him to finish a meeting. Alexa overheard us talking, popped her head around the corner, and said, "Hey, I can take you home."

That simple offer sparked a long, deep, and meaningful friendship. From that day forward, whenever I was working in the city, Alexa became my ride to and from work. Her life was full of family and other responsibilities, but Alexa always made time for me.

You might think that getting to work in Bermuda would be a quick thing, given the entire country is less than twenty-one square miles. However, some days it could take an hour to drive to town. During those long drives, we talked about everything under the sun!

Alexa was a straight shooter who told me what I needed to hear, not what I wanted to hear. I knew I could count on her to give me caring advice.

As I matured, it was no longer a mentor-mentee relationship—we became close friends. Alexa even joined a Tribe that I started, which still exists twenty years later. As a result, there was nothing more natural than to have Alexa by my side on one of the most important days of my life: my wedding.

For some odd reason, my wedding ceremony was running late. My planner said, "Sit tight. We are not ready to start yet."

To distract me, I asked Alexa a question, "Hey, Alexa, today is one of the most important days of my life. What advice or words of wisdom do you have for me?"

Given it was my wedding day, I was expecting to hear, "Don't go to bed angry, make him your best friend, and date often." You know the standard newlywed advice.

Instead, Alexa surprised me. She looked me straight in my eyes and said, "Leah, over the years, your relationships will take different paths. Some of the friends you had for years will drift away. Some will drift away, but then come back, and there will be new friends who will come into your life. The key is just to be open."

Of course, I thanked her. But I remember thinking, as my dad took my hand and we started down the aisle, that it was odd advice for a wedding day. Little did I know those words would continue to resurrect themselves at critical moments for years to come.

Fast-forward five years to my son's third birthday when our house overflowed with fifty family members and friends. You might think: "Why so many people for a three-year-old's party?"

My husband and I always knew there would be times when our children would need other people, voices to give them wise counsel and invest in them. I was not consciously building a Tribe for them at the time, but I innately wanted to surround them with people who would always have their backs.

There we were: Winnie-the-Pooh decorations, loud music, food, laughter, and games spilled from every corner of the house. Alexa was there. However, she was quiet, not laughing. I could see in her eyes that something was not quite right. With so many people around, it was difficult to find a good time to talk, but I made a mental note to call her and check in.

The next day I asked: "Alexa, how are you feeling? You did not seem like yourself at the party."

Alexa brushed me off, "I'm just tired."

Feeling a little uneasy, but not knowing what else to say, I encouraged her to rest.

The following week it was the same. "I don't know. I'm just tired."

A few days later I was preparing to head over to her house when I got a call: "Alexa is at the hospital."

That call changed everything. Alexa's world spiraled into an emergency trip overseas, followed by testing, and visit after visit to medical experts. I flew to Boston to support her family, be with her, and hold her hand. Then, less than four weeks later, Alexa was gone.

I was emotionally unprepared for the loss. Losing Alexa was one of the hardest things I have ever endured. Her sudden passing, in the prime of her life, with three teenagers who desperately needed her, when I needed her, left me broken with an aching emptiness. I was angry, confused, and struggling to understand why our larger-than-life, loving, vibrant wife, mother, and friend was taken from us.

The older I get, the more I understand what a special gift a Tribe can be. This gift became even more evident to me when our Tribe said a sad and emotional goodbye to Alexa. Something was comforting about having a Tribe who understood my pain. I was not alone.

With tears streaming down my face, I tossed a flower onto the gravesite as my final goodbye, and Alexa's wedding-day wisdom to "be open" rang true. Her wise counsel: "Some friends will drift away" and "New friends will come in," reminded me that even though I could not imagine how I would live without her, eventually I would be okay.

I share this story about my dear friend because she was right. Life is short and can take swift and unexpected turns. It's my sincere hope that as we explore *Assemble the Tribe*, our mindsets will shift to be different, be more open. In doing so, we will create a world where no woman, no girl, and by extension, no life that we touch, should ever feel alone.

UNLOCKING THE FORMULA

How do we find this new values system that brings us closer together? I have found that Tribe is more than just people who physically come together. In its most elevated state, Tribe is a mindset, a way of thinking, which is embodied in my simple formula:

BELIEVE
If we believe in our value as human beings

BELONG
and have found any place to belong

BE DIFFERENT
we can leverage our belief and belonging to be OPEN to new relationships and THRIVE in the relationships we have

As we digest this formula, we might be thinking, *I am still not sure I understand what it means to be different.* When most of us consider being different, we think about the attributes and qualities that make us unique—gender, race, hair color, sense of style, personality, beliefs, skills, etc. It is important to remember that Tribe, at its highest level, is a mindset. That means that for each part of the formula, it's about being intentional and different in the way that we think.

When engaging in relationships, every day, we have to make conscious choices to show up differently. Think about it like this: if we wanted to lose ten pounds, our nutrition knowledge and exercise techniques might help us to lose weight more efficiently. Ultimately it's the mindset and the resolve that we have to get up and do something differently each day that will help us to lose the weight.

The same holds true with how we think about engaging in relationships. Daily, we have to make a conscious choice and say, "Today, I am going to be kinder, more open to whomever I meet and do my best to be a better friend, colleague, spouse, sister, mother, etc." That is when we are at our best, being different and thriving with a new tribe mindset.

This formula guides how we leverage our relationships to interact more positively with everyone who comes into our sphere of influence. Worst-case scenario, the relationship does not work, and we are rejected. However, we can survive when we have belief in our value and have found belonging. Best-case scenario, we will connect with a like-minded person(s) and add them to our Tribe.

According to Staci Danford, a gratitude neuroscientist and CEO of The Gratitude Business, "The mind and the brain work simultaneously but are separate. Our brains process our life experiences, but it's our mindset and the stories we tell ourselves that create our reality. The brain is our hardware, but it needs the software of our mind to function."

When we adopt a Tribe mindset, this new way of thinking about relationships, we load new software into our brains. This new software tells us to think differently about our individual value and how we find belonging and connection.

REMEMBER

A Tribe is made up of individually complex people with shared beliefs, values, or interests, who choose to come together in various ways (physical, virtual, informal) to create relationships. Anyone whom you choose can become part of your Tribe.

In its most elevated state, Tribe is a mindset captured in the simple formula: Believe + Belong = Be Different. We have to load this new mindset formula into our brains, be open, and change the stories we tell ourselves about our value and our relationships.

REFLECT

- Do you think you have a Tribe mindset? If not, do you want one? How might having a Tribe mindset benefit you?
- Finding tribes can be hard. Spend some time thinking about where you find your belonging. List all the various Tribes you currently have and name the people who belong to each. If you don't currently have a Tribe, what Tribe would you create first, and who might belong to it?

BE DIFFERENT

Having a Tribe mindset means you *believe* that you have value, and if you have found ANY place to *belong*, then you have the capacity to *be different*, more open in all of your relationships. Consider the ways you might adopt this mindset in your day-to-day interactions.

CHAPTER 2

THE BENEFITS OF TRIBE

RELATIONSHIPS IMPACT OUR HEALTH

From the moment we are born to the day we die, there's something deep within us that yearns for connection. It's not just about the number of people in our lives or even the number of friends or likes we get on social media. Our life experiences are more enjoyable when people decide to sink deep roots into our lives and stay for the long haul.

In 1964, Nelson Mandela was sentenced to life in prison along with eight other African National Congress leaders. Convicted of sabotage and conspiracy to overthrow the government, he was imprisoned for twenty-seven years, eighteen of those years on Robben Island. Mandela and the other prisoners were utterly isolated in solitary confinement. In his autobiography, Mandela wrote, "I found solitary confinement the most forbidding aspect of prison life. There was no end and no beginning; there's only one's own mind, which can begin to play tricks."[4]

When he was not in solitary confinement, it was the community Nelson created who helped him to survive. Gay McDougall, director of an organization that assisted thousands of political prisoners in South Africa, knew Nelson Mandela. She said, "One of the things that was extraordinary about Mandela is his sense that being in a group...of people...is an essential element in movement building and survival in circumstances that are harsh and oppressive."[5]

This is a sad but profound example demonstrating that even amid tough circumstances, finding and connecting with people can have a meaningful impact on our ability to survive. According to a University of Austin study by Debra Umberson, PhD, professor of sociology, and Jennifer Karas Montez, professor of sociology, social relationships can have short-term and long-term effects on our health, for better and for worse. These effects emerge in childhood and cascade throughout life to foster cumulative advantages or disadvantages for our health.

In my experience and research, I have identified several indicators of low-and high-quality relationships:

High-Quality Relationships	Low-Quality Relationships
Low conflict/stress	High conflict/stress
Meaningful time investment	No/limited time investment
Love/caring actions	Indifference/lack of care
Encourage healthy lifestyle behaviors	Encourage negative lifestyle behaviors

We are more likely to live longer, fulfilled lives if we have quality relationships that sustain us emotionally. Lower-quality relationships can lead to higher instances of illnesses such as high blood pressure, cancer, and increased risk of mortality.[6]

In addition to relationship quality, our ability to connect matters as well. A 2015 study conducted by psychologist Julianne Holt-Lunstad and colleagues looked at the data of 3.4 million people across seventy studies. The study found that we expose ourselves to significant health risks when we are lonely or socially isolated. Loneliness, social isolation, and living alone increases the likelihood of death by 29 percent on average.[7]

Two additional studies examined the impact social relationships have on breast cancer survival rates. The first study was conducted on a group of 9,267 women. It found that women who are socially isolated are 43 percent more likely to experience breast cancer recurrence, and 65 percent are more likely to experience breast cancer mortality. The study also found that socially isolated women are more likely to have lower levels of physical activity, drink more than recommended, smoke, and be obese.[8]

The second study examined the association of quality of life of approximately 2,200 women in China after the diagnosis of breast cancer with mortality and recurrence. In an interview, the lead researcher Dr. Meira Epplein said: "The biggest surprise was that physical well-being was less important than strong social ties in breast cancer outcomes."[9]

The results found that women with the highest quality of social well-being (marriage, family, friends) had a 38 percent reduced risk of mortality and a 48 percent lower risk that cancer would recur. According to the research, the strongest benefits for improved survival came from social well-being in the first year after diagnosis.[10]

When I spoke to Dr. Epplein, Associate Professor of Population Health Sciences at Duke University and Co-Leader of the Cancer Control and Population Sciences Program in the Duke Cancer Institute, she said: "When women are diagnosed with breast cancer, the research shows that it is critically important that they have a strong social support network within that first year. While social well-being can be developed post-diagnosis, as women, we will be better positioned to navigate the impact if we build and invest in our social networks and Tribes beforehand."

Dr. Epplein went on to say, "There is so much valuable research available today about how our social connections and quality of life improve longevity and health outcomes. My hope is that as researchers and medical professionals, we can continue to share the results of our studies with increasingly wider audiences and impact more lives."

POSITIVE PEER PRESSURE MATTERS

If we allow them, our Tribes can expose us to positive peer pressure on many dimensions. Our Tribes might encourage us to try new things, travel, embark on new experiences, and support us when we need to make meaningful life changes. Our Tribes can also have a positive impact on our physical and mental health.

Research shows that our social ties can cause us to feel a greater sense of concern for others, which leads us to take actions that encourage better health outcomes for others and ourselves. For example, high blood pressure (HBP) runs in my family. When my parents or siblings reach out and share what they are doing to manage their HBP, I am more inclined to listen and proactively take steps to stay healthy. Conversely, our social ties can have a negative influence on us as well. For example, obesity substantially increases for those who have an obese spouse or friends.[11]

I will never forget after the birth of my two kids. I was thirty pounds overweight and feeling somewhat depressed. After months of not feeling good about myself, my husband and I decided to put ourselves on a structured plan. It just so happened that same year, at least four of my girlfriends decided to make some life changes as well. We all chose different programs, but what was really powerful was the sharing and "positive peer pressure." We spent time talking about our journeys, what was working, and things that were a complete flop. We sometimes exercised together and organized healthy meals when our families got together.

In the end, our weight loss ranged from twenty to more than fifty pounds. The impact on our health was tremendous: blood pressure and blood sugar levels were lowered, and injuries disappeared. This was a great example of how leaning into our Tribes can dramatically increase lifestyle success.

The same study by Dr. Debra Umberson, PhD, and Jennifer Karas Montez also highlighted that our happiness can be impacted or spread through our social networks.[12]

I have a friend who is one of the most positive people you could ever meet. A year ago, she was in a deep personal health and family crisis. However, in the midst of it all, she was able to maintain a hopeful, positive, and happy spirit. Just being in her presence was incredibly inspiring. Her happy outlook helped those around her to think more positively about the challenges we tackled every day. I have also found that celebrating successes and encouraging each other can shift the tone and atmosphere in relationships.

TRIBES MATTER PROFESSIONALLY AND PERSONALLY

The Tribes we form at work impact our health as well. Another study published by the Society for Personality and Social Psychology highlighted: "Health at work is determined to a large extent by our social relationships in the workplace and, more particularly, the social groups we form there."

The research reviewed fifty-eight studies covering people in a variety of occupations, from service and health to sales and military work, in fifteen countries. According to lead researcher Dr. Niklas Steffens, "We are less burnt out and have greater well-being when our team and our organization provide us with a sense of belonging and community when it gives us a sense of 'we-ness.'"[13]

I once worked with an incredible team. While we had our ups and downs, I have never seen a team pull together and work as hard as we did. I remember on one occasion, we were working on a critical time-sensitive project. Everyone was delirious and pulling between ten- and sixteen-hour days.

One day I called a team member for a quick check-in. To my shock and surprise, when I logged into the video conference, she was wearing shades. Before I could get a word out, she said, "Leah, I am so sorry, I am so sorry; I know I look horrendous and unprofessional, but I have been staring at the screen for so many hours that I can hardly open my eyes!" She then started to apologize profusely again. I stopped her and said, "Hold on."

I reached into my handbag and pulled out my shades, put them on, turned back to the screen, and said, "No problem—we will just conduct this meeting with shades!"

Immediately following that call, we had to jump on our weekly team call. Before we logged on, I asked everyone from the team to put on their shades. We logged into the video conference with shades, and our colleague nearly fell out of her chair. As you can imagine, we had *the* best laugh and a great meeting!

What strikes me now as I look back, even in the midst of a crushing schedule, is that everyone chipped in and we still found a way to laugh. I have worked with a lot of great teams, but the "we-ness" I experienced with that team will forever be one of the highlights of my career.

Last but not least, we might be inclined to say, "I have my family; I don't need new relationships." But according to a 2017 study by William J. Chopik of Michigan State University involving nearly 280,000 people, he found that investments in both family and friend relationships are associated with greater health and happiness overall. However, only valuing friendships became a stronger predictor of health and happiness as one ages.[14]

The study was not suggesting that family relationships do not matter. Rather, it was making the point that family relationships can come with emotional stress and, therefore, can have less of a healthy role, but families still matter. The study highlighted that the natural family stresses and strains that occur, such as making difficult long-term care decisions for parents, make familial relationships more complicated, particularly as we age.

When we are feeling stressed or managing through a difficult situation, we may have a natural tendency to isolate ourselves. It's time to shift that way of thinking and lean into our Tribes for support, whether at home or work.

REMEMBER

Our Tribes can have incredible benefits. If we want to live longer, healthier, happier lives, we have to find and maintain quality relationships personally and professionally.

REFLECT

- List the top five "relationships" in your life. Using the relationship quality assessment grid in this chapter, for each person, assess each measure of relationship quality on a scale of 1 (poor quality) to 5 (high quality).
- Do you have quality relationships at home, in your personal life, and at work? If not, why not? What needs to happen in order to create more of them?

BE DIFFERENT

- If you rated the quality of any of your relationships 3 or below, write down one or two ways you can improve the dynamics of the relationship and proactively take action.
- Consider having a conversation with the individuals on your list about how they view your relationship quality. Ask them for suggestions on what it would take to make the relationship even stronger.

CHAPTER 3

WHY *ASSEMBLE THE TRIBE* OF WOMEN?

There are many great movies about the complexity and strength of females. Each of us can probably name a few with female leads and casts. The top movies that come to mind for me include *Hidden Figures, The Sisterhood of the Traveling Pants, Charlie's Angels, Waiting to Exhale, The First Wives Club, Little Women, A League of Their Own,* and *Steel Magnolias.*

The characters articulate the complex layers and lives of women. As I stuffed popcorn into my mouth and the plots unfolded, even if I was not fully aware at the time, on reflection, I can now see a little of myself in each movie. I saw my strength and courage. I saw my relationships and ability to connect people and Tribes for good. However, I could also see the issues I perpetuated because of fear or insecurity. In other moments, I felt sadness as I acknowledged the stereotypes and limitations that others had projected onto me. At times, I was embarrassed and ashamed by the pain I willingly or unknowingly inflicted on others.

As we reflect on these movies, the good news is that they give us hope. Hope that when we as women shift our mindsets and come together to support each other, as friends or even casual acquaintances, our lives can be different, better.

As I wrote this book, time and time again I asked myself, "Leah, the processes and benefits of finding a Tribe are not gender-specific, so why write a book for women?"

When I reflected more deeply, I found my reasons are personal, historical, and scientific.

WHY IS IT PERSONAL?

The need for a book intended to speak about women's relationships is first and foremost personal. When I think back on my involvement with females and female groups over time, my experience was a mixed and sometimes bumpy road—bumps I sometimes created myself.

In my teens and early twenties, at times I was excluded, and it hurt. At other points, I was a bystander, and as I watched relationships unfold, I saw negative behavior driven by hormones, groupthink, and cliques. I saw friendships destroyed and mixed groups splintered when the females "could not get along." These were things I wanted to avoid.

In more recent years, I have seen strong female relationships and groups develop. This was incredibly empowering and inspiring to watch. I have also counseled friends and cried with them as their spirits were crushed by the loss of important friendships. With a heavy heart, I have watched these women float around like an empty bottle, often at the expense of emotional and physical health, while trying to make sense of the loss.

Even in mixed groups, female relationships are different. In my experience, when couples get together, the needs of the women in the group differ. I have seen several mixed groups splinter because the females could not get along. All the while, the males stood by and watched, most feeling helpless or unwilling to wade into the fray.

I am 100 percent sure my younger self would have appreciated a window into the complexity of women while trying to navigate the world. As we look into society today, we see ever-increasing incidents of nationalism, divisions, and adult isolation. Our teens struggle with increasing incidents of bullying, depression, anxiety, lack of self-acceptance, and trust. Against this back-drop, I believe the call to action is clear and critical.

If there's anything we can do as women to enhance our under-standing of each other and build stronger bridges in our families, friend circles, and communities, the time is now. I know as a mom raising two preteen kids, one of whom is a young girl, I sure intend to try.

THE HISTORY OF WOMEN

It's impossible to write about the importance of female relation-ships without delving into the legacy women bring to the table and the complex tapestry that shapes the female experience. The role of women in society has continually evolved since the beginning of time. Throughout history, women are seen as strong rulers, warriors, powerful priestesses, and political leaders.

For example, Cleopatra ruled in ancient Egypt from 52 to 31 BC, Joan of Arc led the French Army in the 1400s, Queen and Warrior Amina of Nigeria ruled the state of Zaria and opened trade routes in the 1500s, and Indira Gandhi was Prime Minister of India in the 1900s.[15] These women are great examples of influential leaders. However, in many ways, these women are the exception. In many societies, past and present, women are thought of as property, inferior, weak, and not equal. As women, sometimes our contributions are overlooked and underappreciated.

Voting rights (in the early 1900s in the United Kingdom and the United States of America) followed by the two world wars brought about change for women. With the men off at war, women were compelled and sometimes forced outside of the home to work in order to survive and keep economies afloat. This new independence had a meaningful impact on how women connected and viewed their roles in society. Some wanted to return to their homes, while others felt it was time to take their rightful place in the workforce.

Over the centuries, societies have defined the role of women and continue to do so today. In many countries, women could not vote, own businesses or own property, and young women were often forced into marriages against their wishes. Even today, equality has not arrived. For example, I recently met a group of women from Saudi Arabia who were excited to have recently been granted the right to drive—something that many of us take for granted every day.

Today the role of women is still evolving. In the business arena, women are on the path to parity. However, there's still a long way to go. According to a 2019 McKinsey study, women representation in the C-Suite stands at 21 percent after more than a decade of focus. Progress to the top of the corporate world continues to be limited by what is called the "broken rung." For every 100 men promoted and hired to management positions, only 72 women were promoted or hired to similar positions. As a result, more women got stuck in entry-level roles. Men ended up holding 62 percent of manager-level positions, while women hold a mere 38 percent.[16]

History reminds us that the role of women in society has always been complex. While we have made great progress in defining what equality looks like, there's still much more progress to be made. As women, we need each other and allies to continue to effect change across the globe for all women.

THE SCIENCE

The battle between nature versus nurture is equally intriguing. From a scientific perspective, I have always been curious as to whether biology or environment influences how we engage in our relationships as women. It's important to note before we venture any further that, when exploring data, there are always exceptions to behavior, and some of this data may not apply to everyone.

NATURE

For the casual eye, it's easy to see there are differences between males and females. From the structure of our bodies to the hormones coursing through our veins, there are differences.

Over the years, the scientific community has amassed numerous studies and reports conducted on both animals and humans that show differences in male and female biology and behavior. For example, there was a study by Oliver Collignon and a team from the University of Montreal demonstrating that women are better at distinguishing between emotions. To develop the conclusions, they hired actors and asked 23 men and 23 women to categorize what they heard and saw as fear or disgust. The study found women were faster in processing emotions overall. The study also showed women were superior in assessing emotions when they were portrayed by a female actor.[17]

Other studies found differences in the biology and behaviors of males and females across a number of dimensions. For example, "Women most often demonstrate an advantage in verbal abilities—particularly verbal fluency, speech production, the ability to decode a language, and spelling; perceptual speed and accuracy; and fine motor skills—whereas men frequently show an advantage on tests of spatial abilities, quantitative abilities, and gross motor strength." Differences have also been found related to childhood play behavior, pain tolerance, frequency of visits to health care professionals, and incidents of mental disorders, just to name a few.[18]

There are thousands of studies highlighting the differences between males and females in terms of biology and behavior. Based on these studies, it's easy to see how our behavior, preferences, and health vulnerabilities have a meaningful impact on the way we approach our relationships. This competing reality of nature versus nurture has, at times, left women with an unavoidable blueprint for our lives. When we as women connect with each other, we create the support and potential opportunity to counteract what could be deemed to be an inevitable path.

WOMEN NEED EACH OTHER

Science also suggests that women have an innate need for female companionship. When women are looking for emotional support, we are still more likely to find kindred spirits with other women. According to the research, even with the known complexities relationships can sometimes bring, women tend to seek each other out.

One landmark study by Laura Klein and Shelley Taylor on relationships found that when life becomes challenging, women seek out friendships. Women "tend and befriend" other women as a means of regulating stress levels.[19]

Female relationships can have a positive impact on our success at work, too. Another recent Harvard study found having a network of professional peers is beneficial for both males and females. The study found that women who have a close circle of female connections are more likely to land executive positions with greater authority and higher pay.[20]

NURTURE

Gender stereotyping is an equally fascinating area of study. For many years, neuroscientists have focused on the concept of brain plasticity or the ability of our brain to form and reorganize synaptic connections in response to learning and experiences. The studies show it's the environment that we live in and expectations of those around us that shape our views. This socialization starts to take place from the moment we are born.[21]

A study by Steven Spencer and his colleagues explored the stereotype differences in math performance. When women and men were given a test with no indication of gender stereotypes, the women performed equal to men. However, the research found that merely telling a woman the math test had produced gender differences caused a notable difference in performance.[22]

Think about some of the stereotypes we see perpetuated in society. We give dolls to our girls and Legos to our boys. Women are more nurturing, while men are more confident or aggressive. Women should be graceful and soft-spoken. while men should be "manly" and strong. When men are forceful, they are seen as strong. When women are forceful, they are sometimes seen as emotional or difficult.

In many households, women still assume the primary caregiver role (children, elderly, household duties), even though they are contributing to the workforce, too. Whether we like it or not, these stereotypes can subconsciously influence how we show up or contribute to relationships, in general, but particularly with women.

RECONCILING IT ALL

As women, we are innately wired to respond in certain ways due to our biology, and then our environment heavily influences us from the time we are born. For each of us, the key is to make intentional choices about how we show up and give in our relationships. Even with natural or social tendencies, we can still choose how we will respond to others and build our relationships.

Assemble the Tribe is for women because we need to think about our story differently. Women comprise nearly 50 percent of the world's population.[23] As a result, women have a tremendous opportunity to influence the world and future generations. We are different—not inferior, just different.

I have written *Assemble the Tribe* for women because our needs and perspectives matter. The impact we have on society is meaningful, and it's time to have a real and different dialogue. It's critical that we create the space to learn and grow together so we can thrive in our relationships today and in generations to come.

REMEMBER

As women, we need each other. Our history, biology, and social experiences impact how we develop and nurture relationships.

REFLECT

- What are some of the social stereotypes you have observed, experienced, or even perpetuated?
- Spend time reflecting on your relationships. What differences have you noticed between men and women in terms of how they relate to each other?

BE DIFFERENT

- Have a conversation with a friend or group about the behaviors and stereotypes impacting your relationships. What can you individually and collectively do differently to break some of the stereotypes you discussed?
- What personal commitments can you make to being more supportive of women in the future?

CHAPTER 4

OUR TRIBES CAN CHANGE OUR DESTINY

A TRIBE STORY

 My name is Ann. Tribes have changed my life. They have impacted my health, provided support, and helped me to dream when I had given up. No matter what, because of them I will forever stay open. This is my Tribe story.

GROWING UP

My first memory of Tribe was observing my mom. When I was young, she didn't have many friends. My dad used to say to her, "You don't need friends; your family are your friends." Later on, when my parents separated, Mom became close with two women. My sister and I followed in her footsteps and had few close friends.

I was a happy, easygoing child. I loved to be around other people, to observe them, engage them in conversation, sit with them, and drink in their stories. But the relationships did not go deep. I was looking for my Tribe.

I CAN'T BREATHE

Fast-forward many years to after my marriage, when the most natural thing in the world would be to one day wake up and say, "Let's have a baby," and we would get pregnant. But that was not my journey at all. I remember the first part of the story happened as planned: my husband and I said, "Come on, let's do this." However, weeks, months, years passed, but for some reason, getting pregnant just wasn't happening.

One night I turned over in bed, touched my stomach, and felt something hard. Somewhat alarmed, I called my doctor, and we went in. The diagnosis: a fibroid. Rather than focusing on a baby, we shifted course and focused on surgery and recovery.

Months later, we looked at each other again and said, "Okay, that's done; let's get pregnant," but again it wasn't happening.

I would read stories about women who had fibroids and had gotten pregnant. I started second-guessing myself: "Maybe we made a bad choice to have the surgery." Even though there was no rationale for it, I started blaming myself for not getting pregnant. To make matters worse, I worked with young children as an Early Childhood Specialist. Every day families came into my office, and because I couldn't get pregnant, it was like pouring salt on an open wound. Some days I felt like I couldn't breathe.

STEPPING OUTSIDE MY COMFORT ZONE

Thankfully, a few years before all of this happened, I found a Tribe who supported me in my pain. One evening we were having ladies' night, and I don't know what came over me, but I became outraged. I said, "I've done everything right all these years, and I still can't have a child!"

Looking back, I was angry because I realized there was a possibility I would never have a child. That thought broke my heart in two. Not wanting to give up, we went to a fertility specialist.

The doctor said, "If you were my daughter, I would encourage you to have in vitro fertilization."

I said, "How much is that going to cost?"

"About $30,000."

"Well, I guess I'm not your daughter because there is no way I can make that happen."

My husband and I held hands and walked out of the doctor's office devastated. My world darkened as reality set in.

Around that time, a friend from my Tribe checked in on me and said, "Hey, come to this Body Combat kickboxing class; let's go get some exercise."

Wanting something to distract me, I said, "Okay. Why not? I might enjoy it. More than likely, I won't, but why not?"

At that point, I was at an all-time weight high. I went to the class with an open mind, thinking, "Okay, let's do this!" I loved Body Combat. In a year, I was down twenty-five pounds. The more I exercised, the better I ate, the more water I drank, and within a short time, I looked and felt fabulous!

TRIBES CAN IMPACT OUR HEALTH AND WELL-BEING

I looked forward to the class. The kickboxing course was a breath of fresh air. The group came from all walks of life, and in it, I found cheerleaders and motivators. We pushed each other to be better.

The instructor set up a chat to keep us connected outside of class. As time went on, our bonds strengthened. As each of us lost weight and met our goals, we celebrated. I was able to push my pain of loss aside. I had found a new Tribe who supported me. We looked out for each other.

In the end, I lost weight, and my stress levels receded. The endorphins made me feel better, and I started going to more classes. It became my passion. As the weight continued to fall away, the pain in my heart eased somewhat, but never entirely went away.

TRIBES CAN CHANGE OUR DESTINY

One fateful fall day, another one-on-one Tribe member stopped by for a short visit. While driving her back to the hotel, she said, "Ann, you look fabulous!"

I sighed, "Yeah," with a sad tone to my voice.

She asked, "Why did you say 'yeah' like that?"

"I feel good, but I wish more than anything I could have a baby."

I was a little surprised by myself. I hadn't spoken to anyone in months about wanting a baby.

She said, "Gee, Ann, I didn't know that was something you wanted."

"Yes. It's just not happening. I thought I was over it, but there are days when I feel like this."

"Can I share something with you?"

Intrigued, I replied, "Sure, go ahead."

"I have a friend in Florida. She's a doctor. A few of my friends have signed up for her program, which includes a combination of natural herbs and vitamins. In fact, a few of them, after a few months, have gotten pregnant. Perhaps you should try them."

A little wary, I said, "I guess I can try them."

Two weeks later, a package arrived with the pills. It was three or four bottles of omegas and other herbal tablets. I started the pills in November. Nothing happened.

Then it did! In February of the following year, amid my busy schedule, I noticed my cycle was a few days late. I thought, "Hmm, that's strange. Something must be up."

I'll never forget. It was like yesterday. It was a Wednesday. I was trying to talk myself into taking the pregnancy test. I put it off because I knew it was a fluke, and I was not ready to deal with any more disappointment. But something kept telling me, "Take the test, Ann. Take the test."

That inner voice was clear. It wasn't a whisper. It was like, "Take the test!" It was so clear. Finally, I gave in and scooped out four boxes of pregnancy tests left over from all the times I had taken them before. I took two. I was on pins and needles as I waited for the first one to come through. It was a faint yes. I picked up the second test, and it showed a bright yes: you're pregnant.

Not ready to believe it, I turned the boxes over to check the expiration dates, which were fine. I said to myself, "This is not accurate. These pregnancy tests were sitting in the dampness. The results are because of the Bermuda weather."

I took two more tests. Both came back positive. Even with four positive results, I still kept saying, "This can't be right!"

I called my doctor's office. My doctor never answers the phone, but on this day, my miracle day, she picked up. I explained to her what transpired.

The doctor said, "Ann, you took four pregnancy tests? Of course, you're pregnant!" But she understood I needed her confirmation. I went in and took a blood test. It confirmed: "Yes, I was pregnant!"

TRIBES HELP US EXPERIENCE MIRACLES

The process of meeting my little girl was a journey in itself. At one point, we weren't sure if I was going to be able to carry her to term. I was off and on bed rest. However, I believe because I had gone to Body Combat, and my body was strong, I was ready for the fight. My body was able to handle a developing baby, competing fibroids, and the pain that came as they collided.

My body seemed to hold her in place, and nine months later, my little miracle daughter was born.

At each stage of the journey, my Combat Tribe was cheering me on, and my sister Tribe and girlfriends were there when I needed them. I believe with all my heart that it was God using my Tribes to help me realize my miracle. Without the invitation, I would not have gone to class. Without support, I would not have lost thirty-plus pounds. Without the vitamins, my body might not have prepared itself. Without support and prayers along the way, I might have given up.

MY JOURNEY OF TRIBE CONTINUES

Today, I am still open. I strive to be my best. And my Tribes still push me to be a better version of myself, a better wife, and a better mother.

In summary, it's been a journey. As with all relationships, there were some issues along the way. However, I've learned that no matter what happens, good, bad, or indifferent, there's always a lesson to learn.

I share my Tribe story because it reminds me of how important it is to allow people into our lives. People can change our destiny, and we can do the same for others when we choose to be different, more caring, more open. I have lived a life of Tribe, experienced a miracle, and I am so thankful.

HERE ARE MY TOP FIVE WAYS TO BE DIFFERENT:

1. **Always Be You:** If somebody's not going to accept you

because you're you, then they might not be the right person to travel life's journey with. That's okay.

2. **Deep Relationships Take Time and Intention:** We all have busy lives, but if we want support, love, and relationship depth, we have to put in the time and be intentional.

3. **Don't Be Quick to Judge:** Sometimes we hastily formulate opinions about people we haven't met or had a conversation with. Don't be quick to cross somebody off your list because of a quirk. We all have idiosyncrasies. That's life. It makes us who we are.

4. **Make Sure Your Belief Systems Align:** It's essential to find a Tribe who shares your beliefs. If I didn't have a Tribe who believed in a God who can do the impossible, I am not sure how I would have made it through.

5. **Have Fun:** There are many things I wouldn't have done if not for my Tribes. I've gone on girls' trips, enjoyed annual vision boarding, and attended concerts. We have experimented with cooking together, flying kites, and on and on. If we are going to live a life of Tribe, we have to have fun in the process.

PART 2

Believe + Belong

CHAPTER 5

LEVEL I

DISCOVERING YOU

The Four Levels of Relationship

Level I. My relationship with myself

Level II. My one-on-one relationships

Level III. My group (3 or more) relationships

Level IV. My relationships with everyone else

IT ALL STARTS WITH YOU

When most of us are ready to begin a relationship, we just do it, jump right in. However, sometimes there are issues inside of us that need sorting out before we should step one foot, even one toe, into a new relationship. If we want to be able to enjoy healthy connections, the first relationship that has to be healthy is the relationship we have with ourselves.

BELIEF: THE BEGINNING OF TRIBE

When we embark on the journey of adding to our Tribes, we first have to consider if we believe we are valuable, worthy of belonging.

At the root of any positive relationship is the belief that we matter—our opinions, views, strengths, and weaknesses matter. We deserve understanding and appreciation. We have to choose to believe this as fact and, if necessary, get help to deeply understand our value.

This belief about our value is what I call a Level I relationship: our relationship with ourselves.

To bring it home, let's explore a real-life example of Cameron, who wants to add to her Tribe. Cameron was rejected by her father as a young child and has a deep belief that she is not enough. Something as simple as a person walking by and not speaking to her may cause her to question her value. On other occasions, someone might minimize her views or opinions. Instead of speaking up, she shrinks back and becomes more withdrawn. This constant situational devaluing triggers a negative mindset and has a detrimental impact on her interactions, relationships, and sense of self-worth.

UNDERSTANDING WHAT MAKES US VALUABLE

A big part of understanding and believing in our value is understanding who we are at our core.

I was eight years old, and my parents were busier than usual on the weekends. As a result, I was unhappy. I missed my mom. A consummate helicopter mom, it was atypical for her to be missing with such regularity. As a result, I decided it was time to have a mother-daughter meeting to discuss what she and my dad were up to. While I can't remember my exact words, here is my adult version of what took place.

> I was eight years old, and I called a meeting! I still smile when my kids do that to us today! It's so essential in our relationships and in raising our kids that we take the time to talk when something does not feel quite right.

While talking to my mother, I discovered that my parents were facilitating a program for married couples at our local church. The program involved classroom training and private counseling sessions with my parents. While helpful, I did not think the explanation provided was enough. I needed to know more.

> As I write this, I am smiling because when my daughter was eight years old, she used to sit me down from time to time to have similar conversations: "How is work? What is your manager's name? What do you do all day? I need details!"

During the inquisition, my mom shared, "As part of the counseling, your dad and I are administering a personality test to help the couples understand each other better."

She explained there are four personality types, and everyone has a dominant and secondary personality type. Each personality type has strengths, and there are inherent weaknesses that could be perceived as negatives by others.

I was intrigued and asked, "Mom, is the test only for adults?"

She paused for a few seconds and said, "I am not sure. I have never given the test to a child before."

"Would it be okay for me to take the test?"

Initially, she said no, but after a few days of nagging, she finally gave in and said, "Let's do it!"

I was so excited. I can still remember sitting down at the table to fill out the form with my little pencil, carefully filling each circle, ensuring that I stayed inside the lines. I couldn't wait to learn something new about myself! After what seemed like hours, my mom scored the test, and it was time to review my results. I could barely contain myself!

Drum roll...I was "Choleric Sanguine," but what on earth did that mean? Remember, I was only eight years old.

My mom explained, "Leah, people with Choleric personalities are born leaders, strong-willed, confident, and can make things happen. Sanguine personalities are talkative, life of the party, and have a good sense of humor."

Mom went on to tell me the rest, "At their worst, Cholerics can be bossy, impatient, and struggle to relax. Sanguines can be restless, too emotional, drive people crazy, and talk too much!"

I was fascinated. For days on end, I peppered my mom with questions about the test:

"What is your personality type?"

"What is my dad's personality type?"

"How do the different personalities impact married couples?"

"Can a personality type change?"

As with most childish pursuits, after a few weeks, the fascination wore off; however, I have never forgotten that test, the four personality types, and my strengths and weaknesses. Thanks to my mom, from a very young age, I understood who I was at my core, both good and bad. I also knew there was something valuable about me that I could give to the world.

Taking the time to explore who we are is the foundation on which we build relationships. If we don't believe we have value and understand who we are, it's difficult to have authentic, healthy relationships.

WHAT DO I HAVE TO GIVE?

Level I is the foundation of all relationships and is where we have to do our most profound work. It's hard and sometimes scary to answer these questions for ourselves: Do I value myself? Who am I? What do I have to give?

The answers can leave us open and raw with feelings of inadequacy and not liking what we see. However, it's the process of exploring who we are that paves the way for clarity. It gives us the confidence to be the best version of ourselves and understand how and where we need to grow.

Here are five mindsets I have found particularly useful when thinking about valuing who we are:

1. **Understanding Our Gifts:** When we know our gifts, talents,

strengths, and personality traits, we have a greater sense of purpose. We can also better appreciate our capacity to impact the world.

2. **Sharing Our Gifts with Others**: A great way to understand our value is to share the best of who we are with others. When we give, and others express their appreciation, it has a cementing effect and reminds us of who we are and that what we have to give does matter.

3. **Remembering That Comparison Kills**: As part of appreciating our value, it's critical to be kind to ourselves by not comparing ourselves to others. There will always be someone who has more: a better singing voice, more hair, fabulous legs, a natural sense of humor, etc., etc., etc. Remember to be kind and love ourselves for who we are and what we have. We will miss out on the best parts of who we are and what we have to give to the world when we spend time wishing for the gifts and talents of someone else.

4. **Practicing Gratefulness**: According to science, gratitude can impact our physical and mental health, sleep, and even self-esteem, just to name a few.[24] The very fact that we have gifts and talents to share to make the lives of others better is something to be grateful for.

5. **Setting Boundaries**: We can also value ourselves by setting boundaries or limits around how we allow others to treat us. I have found that people do to us what we allow. When we create a personal or professional boundary by speaking up for ourselves, that is when we can truly feel empowered and free in who we are.

Don't be afraid to do the work to discover who you are, and don't be scared to get help if you need it. You may not love what you find, but take comfort in the fact that you are searching, which means growth is happening. It's in your quest for personal clarity that you open the door to change and a deeper, more fulfilling life as you move toward the next levels of relationship.

REMEMBER

A strong belief in our value and appreciation of our unique gifts, talents, and strengths are the foundation for establishing healthy relationships.

REFLECT

- List the top three strengths, gifts, or talents you believe you bring to the world.
- How do you apply them in a way that provides value or services to others?
- List ways you compare yourself to others. How can you accept, appreciate, and embrace your own unique abilities and traits?
- What are you currently most grateful for in your life? How could you express your gratitude for these things on a daily basis?
- What healthy boundaries are currently in place that help you live a good life? What boundaries need to be put in place for you to live an even better life?

BE DIFFERENT

Review your answers to the five questions above. Identify at least three to five concrete actions you will take to value yourself even more. Write them down and store them in a place where you can see them often.

CHAPTER 6

LEVEL I

OWNING YOUR "STUFF"

The Four Levels of Relationship

Level I. My relationship with myself

Level II. My one-on-one relationships

Level III. My group (3 or more) relationships

Level IV. My relationships with everyone else

A huge part of relationship development lies in our ability to trust. The first relationship that requires trust is the relationship we have with ourselves. While we might believe and trust that we have value, we also have our own "stuff."

"Stuff" is both internal and external. Internal stuff could be character flaws, personality traits, biases, and other areas of our lives that still need polish and work. External stuff is how we respond to the stereotypes, external voices, beliefs, and opinions others have of us. It's impossible to be the best versions of ourselves when we are not willing to pull our "stuff" out of the back of the closet, wash it, put some starch on it, and make it ready for wear.

When it comes to relationships, we tend to focus on the other person's "stuff" and mask our own as if we can do no wrong. On one level, we want to give, and on another level, we can be defensive and innately selfish. Think about it: When we get ready to enter into a new relationship, do we always take time to reflect on our motivations? Do we go in prepared to give as much as we plan to take from it?

One of the greatest gifts we can give ourselves is the gift of raising our self-awareness about who we are internally and externally in our interactions. We have value, but we are not perfect. To be human is to be flawed, and to this, there's no exception. Personal awareness will get us out of trouble; it will keep us from repeating hard lessons. Awareness will endear us to people as it will likely make each of us a more thoughtful person.

Wherever we are on our Tribe journey, it's essential to take the time to analyze our "stuff." Even when we are ready to jump right into a new relationship, it's possible that our prior experiences have left us scarred, scared, and not prepared.

This chapter will require us to look in the mirror. We know how it goes—some days we wake up, look in the mirror, and we don't always like what we see.

There are so many ways to raise our self-awareness. However, in the context of relationship building, here are four critical

lessons that can keep us mindful of who we are and how we show up in relationships.

MIRROR, MIRROR ON THE WALL—LOOKING INSIDE
LESSON 1—UNDERSTANDING OUR STUFF

Ever since I took my first personality assessment at eight years old, I have eaten up any evaluation, book, or training that helps me understand myself and people better. For example, I have learned there's a difference between my personality, my strengths, and the way I think.

Personality

I will never forget taking my second personality assessment in college with a friend. We received our results in two separate classes. When we compared notes, we discovered that we had some of the same personality traits. I remember her exclaiming to me: "No way! There's no way you and I are the same!"

You see, when we were together, both of us couldn't be "in charge." When I was with her, I chose to take a step back and let her drive. It's important to resist falling into the trap of "that's just who I am, so deal with it." We can, if we work at it, develop personal versatility and maturity and relate better to those around us.

Strengths

As a teenager and then in college, I was always phenomenal at organizing stuff. At one point, I was angry about that. Ideally, we want to be the funniest, the best at a sport, the best writer, I mean, who wants to be the best at organizing work and people?

I thought something was wrong with me. I figured I was just a workaholic who didn't know how to enjoy life. Thankfully, I learned that one of my greatest strengths is to take on a significant number of tasks at once and get them all done. While it might scare some, it gave me energy.

The critical thing about strengths is that when we drive too far or too fast in any direction, these elements can become a liability. For example, I am driven, responsible, love doing lots of things at once, want to achieve, and have no issues pushing others to want more or do more. Imagine if I maxed out on these strengths every day. I might either wear myself out with tasks and to-do lists or annoy everyone around me. Today, I think I am doing much better in this department. My husband and kids will probably tell you I am still in recovery!

The Way We Think

We also have a natural way of processing data and information in our minds. I, for example, see the world through processes and people. My husband, on the other hand, tends to be less verbose, very logical, and analytical. Imagine the conversations we have—let's say, for example, when we are trying to paint the house. I wanted to talk about the meaning of the color and the experience that we wanted people to have in the room. My husband, on the other hand, wanted to know if it's blue, teal blue, gray-blue, or whatever blue so he can get on with painting! There's no right or wrong way to process information, but we have to be mindful that different ways of thinking do have an impact on our relationships.

LESSON 2—WE HAVE TO LEARN TO FLEX

If we are not clear on our personality, how we thi
strengths, we may want to spend some time refl
exploring this part of who we are. There are all kir
and assessments to give us insight. I don't believe these tools
are always 100 percent accurate, but the assessments can give
us perspective and insights that we may not have considered
before. When we don't understand who we are and what we
have to offer in our relationships, we may unintentionally and
subconsciously damage them.

Once we understand more about how we are wired, we can then
learn how to be flexible. Just because we can, does not mean
we should. When we don't learn to flex and consider the traits,
ways of thinking, and strengths of others, our relationships may
not flourish. If we decide not to be flexible, we also need to be
careful not to blame anyone else.

For example, in my house both of the men in my family are
very relaxed and do not use many words. I, on the other hand,
prefer to talk with more color! For instance, this is a normal
afternoon conversation with my son:

Me: "Hi, how was your day at school?"

My son: "Fine."

Me: "Did anything interesting happen today?"

My son: "No."

Me: "What did you learn in science class today?"

My son: "Not much."

Me: "But what did you learn, even if it was not much?"

My son: "The structure of the flower."

I could go on, but you get the picture. As someone who prefers to talk with much more detail and examples, this line of conversation drives me a little crazy. However, I have learned that with my husband and my son, fewer words are king. I have had to learn to be flexible and accept them as they are; less is more. I also have a very chatty girl who keeps me sane, so it works!

 When we take the time to get to know ourselves deeply, we can do more, give more, and help more. The key is to know ourselves and our stuff.

"STUFF" CAN CONNECT US OR DISCONNECT US— LOOKING FROM THE OUTSIDE
LESSON 3—WE CHOOSE HOW WE RESPOND

Sometimes we are going along living life, doing our best, and then life throws a wrench at us and creates changes we didn't see coming.

I was having the time of my life in college. I loved meeting new people, getting involved in campus activities, running the gym, and going to networking events. I was everywhere and loved every minute. I got good grades, was in excellent health, and enjoyed my friends.

One night I was relaxing in my apartment watching the news

when I received a phone call. I picked up the phone and said lightly, cheerfully, "Hello."

On the other end of the line was a classmate who called to talk. Somehow the conversation quickly transitioned from an easygoing hello to a hostile monologue that ended with, "I hate you, I just hate you!" ringing in my ears.

I was completely stunned, speechless, and hurt, while sitting there with the phone in my hand. I began to shake as the tears ran down my face.

If that were to happen to me today, there would be no tears or speechlessness. I would either engage in a conversation or simply let it roll off my back. However, at the age of nineteen or twenty, there was part of me that still needed validation, so the words cut deep.

Before that call, I was naturally driven to be out in front. I loved it. It gave me energy. More than twenty years later, the details of the call are fuzzy. Still, I am sure it was my drive and personality that precipitated the hate. However, that five-minute call had a profound impact on my confidence.

For several years after I left college, I intentionally looked for lower-profile activities. I never wanted to put myself out there so someone, or a group of people, could hurt me like that again. For years I carried that pain with me. However, as they say, time heals all wounds, and eventually I got to the place where I knew I had to let go of all that "stuff" and just be me. I promised myself I would never again let anyone change my perspective about who I am and what I have to give the world.

The bottom line is we can't control how people feel, what they think, and what they say. However, we can control how we choose to respond and if we allow them to change our internal narrative. We have to believe in our value and trust that value no matter what.

LESSON 4—WE ARE NOT EVERYONE'S CUP OF TEA, AND THAT'S OKAY

The final big lesson I have learned is that sometimes, a relationship is not a good fit. Most people naturally prefer to get along with everyone, but sometimes connections with people just don't align. I remember after that hate-filled college phone call, I traveled home and ran into a woman whom I respected and looked up to. I thought she and I shared a proactive belief about mentorship, so I asked her to lunch.

We met at a lovely restaurant overlooking the harbor and started to chat about school and life. She immediately made me feel comfortable, and our banter was light and easy. During the early part of the conversation, she asked me, "Tell me about you and school."

I was a little reluctant, even shy, partially because of that phone call, and I don't like talking about myself. However, I acquiesced and shared my story. She reciprocated and shared her career story, with high transparency about her struggles. I left that lunch appreciative of the honesty and the bond I felt we started to form during the time together.

A few days later, a mutual friend asked me about this lunch. I told her, "The lunch date was so honest and helpful. I am so glad we went to lunch."

She paused and looked at me slightly confused and then shared this: the woman I had lunch with had told her, "Leah is arrogant and full of herself."

I can't tell a lie. This interaction, on the heels of my college experience, cut me very deep, as I was still processing my feelings and was somewhat vulnerable. I thought we had a mutually honest and open conversation, and then to find out she left with that opinion and shared it with others—that really hurt.

My first instinct was to keep feeling hurt, but my second instinct was self-reflection. Was I arrogant? Did I say too much?

In the end, I decided the answers were no and yes. My sharing about my background was not arrogant, but factual. However, when she asked about me, I gave her my "whole story," which for the first meeting was too much.

What I learned as a result of that experience is when getting to know someone, sometimes we have to share in bite-size pieces and let the relationship reveal the rest over time. If not, we could be perceived as something we are not. I never reached out to her again for mentoring, but we naturally connected at various business events. In the end, I chose not to hold that moment against her, even though it had a profound impact on my life for years. Sometimes when we meet new people, it's just not a good fit, and that's okay!

LEAN INTO IT

Sometimes the best gift we can give to ourselves is to lean into the pain and raise our levels of self-awareness about our "stuff." Stuff could be who we are: our personalities, the way we think, or our strengths. Stuff can also mean how we show up in relationships and how we allow those interactions to shape us. When we fail to focus on our "stuff," we miss out on the learning moments that help to perfect the only meaningful thing we take with us through our lives: our character.

When we hide from our hurt and pain and isolate ourselves, we may close relationship doors. As a result, there are people who need us whom we will never meet or touch.

REMEMBER

Raise your level of self-awareness so you can trust yourself and others can trust you, too. How people respond to you can help to refine your character. Take the parts that fit and discard the pieces that don't.

REFLECT

- Find a few minutes and take some time to self-reflect. Are there areas in your personality, the way you think, or strengths that negatively impact your relationships? Write these down.
- Spend a few days thinking about your list. Write down five to ten actions that you can take to shift or change those traits or behaviors.
- Can you think of examples where either you have failed to flex to someone else's style or they failed to flex to yours? What was the impact of failing to be flexible?

BE DIFFERENT

Strive to be self-aware. How are you showing up in your relationships? How are you impacting others? Find someone who loves you and wants the best for you. Ask the individual for feedback on where you could do better, be better. Let them lovingly affirm you and open your eyes to blind spots you may not know are there.

CHAPTER 7

LEVEL II

PUTTING MYSELF "OUT THERE" ONE-ON-ONE

The Four Levels of Relationship

Level I. My relationship with myself

Level II. My one-on-one relationships

Level III. My group (3 or more) relationships

Level IV. My relationships with everyone else

During my research for this book, I talked to many people who struggle to find new connections. Others were heartbroken when they lost relationships because of distance or misunderstandings and were exhausted with the idea of starting over.

There are so many great books that explore how to connect, influence, and build networks. I won't try to cover it all in one short chapter. However, I will share a few tried and tested techniques I have used over the years. Hopefully, these examples will help as we try to get past the scary hurdle of finding one-on-one relationships to add to our Tribes.

A LITTLE FISH IN A BIG POND

Bermuda is a relatively small country. If you were born on the island, you are related to what feels like half the island, and if needed, you can find someone who knows the other half. The population is just that small. If I wanted to find out the details of someone's life, it was so easy to investigate and get the scoop. I mean, with a few phone calls, in a matter of minutes, I could unearth someone's entire life story: who their parents and siblings were, where they attended school, what their belief systems were. If I dug deep, I could find out what they liked for breakfast, lunch, and dinner. No, seriously. In our small community, it was easy to find out information, so that when you connected with a new person, it felt safe.

However, when I moved to New York City for college and work, figuring out how to expand my relationship network was a big challenge. I remember saying to myself at one point, "In this huge city with millions of people, how is it possible that one could feel so alone?"

I had a few friends, but in my quest for independence, I moved out of the dorm, forty-five to sixty minutes away from school. At twenty-one years old, I had to figure out a way to put myself out there and find my Tribe in a way that felt safe.

The thing is, starting over can be a bit daunting, particularly for people who are introverts or ambiverts (someone who displays introverted and extroverted tendencies).

According to the research company Barna Group, the majority of adults in the U.S. have two to five close friends. Still, one in five people report they regularly or often feel lonely. The research cites that those who are not working or work remotely, struggle with loneliness.[25]

The Barna study goes on to reveal that most Americans are friendly but lonely. Surprisingly, the highest percentage of people (42 percent) meet their friends at work, while the rest meet people through other friends (35 percent) or in their neighborhoods (29 percent). The research also found that opposites don't attract, with the majority of people indicating their friends were mostly similar to them. This fact was true regardless of religious beliefs, race, or ethnicity, income, education, social status, political views, or life stage. However, in another research study, Barna found when we have friendships with people who are different from us, we are more empathetic. We also tend to shift our views in positive ways.[26]

What was fascinating in this study was that this pattern of opposites does not exist in the same way for teenagers. Most teens (81 percent) say they often or occasionally interact with people who do not share or do not understand essential parts of their identity. Nearly two-thirds (63 percent) indicate they enjoy spending time with people who are not like them.[27]

As a non-American, I can't say with 100 percent authority that these patterns hold true in every country and nationality. However, the data is instructive in terms of how we think about building new friendships and raising our children: Will we look for the same, or will we step out and look for something different? Given that children and teens are more open to differences, how might we expose them to more diverse environments?

BACK TO THE BIG POND

Not really knowing what to do to build relationships in the big city, I followed my gut instincts. With my mother's "don't go off by yourself with strangers!" ringing loudly in my ears, I began my quest. I started by attending large networking conferences and events and made a concerted effort to put myself out there. When I found someone who I clicked with or found interesting, I made an effort to follow up with coffee or lunch. Then leveraging that newfound relationship, after I felt safe, I was able to ask for referrals, expand my circle, and find new connections.

How did it work practically? There was no one formula. I tried all kinds of things. For example, one of the things I struggled with in New York was how to find the right salon for my hair. I am sure most of you can empathize—finding the right hairdresser is right up there with needing Wi-Fi!

From time to time, the college would sponsor students to attend industry events. One holiday season, a friend and I signed up to attend an awards dinner. It was a very posh, sophisticated affair with men in tuxedos and women in beautiful gowns. As a relatively poor college student, I felt slightly out of place at the elegant event, knowing no one other than my friend. She was just over five feet tall, but a force of nature, funny, focused, and ambitious.

That night she dragged me from one company-sponsored room to the next. She wanted to experience every moment and meet new people, even more than I did. As the evening wore on, we saw two elegant women with the most stunning hair that we had ever seen. We stopped in our tracks. I remember saying to my friend, "I wonder who styles their hair?"

Had it been left up to me, I would have kept moving, but not my friend. She marched me down the hall, and after twenty minutes of chatting, we found out the two ladies were senior executives at a French insurance company.

They were very gracious and invited us to visit them at their offices. From that moment forward, they were always available for a quick chat or advice. I am so thankful for their investment in us. One of the women, more than twenty years later, remains a good friend and mentor today. It's incredible how chance encounters can add so much richness to our lives. I shudder to think that I would have missed out on the chance for a beautiful friendship had it not been for my friend dragging me down that hallway. This story often reminds me to push outside of my comfort zone and connect with people. We never know where chance encounters will lead. Let me just add that, as a result of that encounter, I found a fantastic hair salon that I visited until the day I moved back to Bermuda!

TEN WAYS TO FIND NEW RELATIONSHIPS

What are some of the ways we can put ourselves out there? Here are the top ten approaches I have used over time:

1. **Ask Friends and Family**: Our friends and family know us the best. I was recently contacted by two amazing women who knew someone in my Tribe. They were great referrals. We had lunch and talked about ways we can partner together in the future. Telling our family and friends, who care about us, what we are looking for and asking them to introduce us to new people in their network is a great way to search for new relationships.
2. **Get to Know Neighbors**: Getting out, going for a walk, and

mingling in our neighborhood can be a great way to find a kindred spirit. When I lived in New York, I joined a neighborhood gym and made a few connections. It was a great way to build a network and learn about the area.

3. **Build a Professional Network:** We spend a lot of hours at the office, or on virtual meetings, so take the time to get to know people. In addition to regular meetings, over the years, I have also booked virtual coffee dates. A virtual coffee date is a simple call just to check in, to be mentored, or to mentor someone else. We can also attend company networking events and make an effort to talk to new people. If we don't like talking or it makes us nervous, prepare a list of questions. Talk about kids, pets, travel plans. Most people enjoy talking about themselves.

4. **Attend Events:** Attend events and conferences. Once a year, when I can, I make an effort to attend a conference or event of some sort to take in new ideas and meet new people. It's a great way to build a Tribe.

5. **Volunteer:** Make a list of your strengths and talents, then find organizations that can benefit from them. Not only does it feel great having volunteered time, but you will likely meet some people who have the same passions.

6. **Leverage Your Hobbies:** Think about the hobbies and activities you enjoy. Then find organizations or classes where you can grow, share, and connect over common interests.

7. **Learn about New Cultures:** Sometimes, we are intrigued by different cultures and traditions. Proactively seek people or organizations to grow and expand your thinking about new cultures and connecting with new people.

8. **Talk to Strangers:** When out and about, smile and strike up a conversation with a stranger. We never know what we might learn or who we might meet. When traveling, talk to

strangers. I tend to have the most fascinating conversations when I open myself up to new people.

9. **Tap into Your Pain:** Think about an issue you are trying to work through or something that causes pain. Then seek out an organization or group of like-minded people who can constructively provide support as you look to manage or conquer the issue.

10. **Go Online:** Not all relationships need to happen in person. You can find thousands of online forums and groups of people who share common interests.

There are so many ways we can connect with others and build our Tribes. While in-person is always ideal, there may be times when distance separates us, or we need to engage in physical distancing. For example, while I was writing this book, the Coronavirus was sweeping across the world, forcing people inside and farther apart. However, even before the virus, I was working from home, so I needed to be creative about ways to connect with people when I could not physically be with them.

Investing in relationships virtually can be a rewarding option. I have a friend and we have a virtual weekly meeting to catch up and talk about business, world issues, and our beliefs. Often it is the highlight of my week. That weekly call has brought us closer together even though we are thousands of miles apart.

Before moving on, I have to add this. The most important thing to remember is to act safely and wisely in interactions with new people. Use common sense and good judgment in terms of how much time and where the time is spent. When I was single, living in New York, I never allowed people into my home or went to their homes alone. I always started with coffee and then progressed to lunches or dinners. The key is to be smart and stay safe.

Last but not least, there are two critical things to remember when putting ourselves out there:

1. ANY RELATIONSHIP WORTH HAVING TAKES WORK

Now and again, we find a person, and we just click. However, healthy relationships and friendships often require investments of time, effort, and emotions (TEE). During one particular phase of my career, I was so busy that I never left the office. I allowed relationships to lapse and never took the time to build new ones; all I did was work. One of my mentors gave me some great practical advice: two calls and a cup of coffee. Two calls and a cup of coffee is a practice whereby, every month, I made at least two calls and found someone to have a cup of coffee with to keep my relationships fresh! If we want to maintain or build new relationships, we have to put in the work.

2. BE INQUISITIVE AND SEEK TO KNOW MORE ABOUT THE OTHER PERSON

When we have a focused agenda of finding new relationships, we may be unintentionally self-absorbed. We tend to be laser-focused on how the relationship will benefit us.

When forming new relationships, it's important to take the time to be deeply curious about the other person:

- What do they love to do?
- What's their background?
- What are they passionate about?

- What gets them up in the morning?
- Where do they come from?

We may find that by being deeply curious about others, it strengthens our connection, increases our empathy, and opens our eyes in new ways.

Depending on our personality and preferences, we may connect with lots of people. Alternatively, we might need to invest lots of time one-on-one or in a smaller group and go deeper. Whatever our preference, the goal is to find people who will add richness to our lives and give us safe places to be ourselves to find belonging.

REMEMBER

Anything worth having requires an investment. Relationships are no exception. To find our Tribes, we have to put ourselves out there. There are numerous ways we can find new connections. We just have to put in the time, effort, and emotion to get out there and make it happen!

REFLECT

- If you are looking for new relationships, spend some time thinking about the type of relationship that will bring richness to your life right now. If it's helpful, write down five to ten attributes you are looking for in a relationship.
- Take a step back and think about your existing, one-on-one relationships and friendships. Do you dedicate enough time to allow the connection to stay healthy or deepen? Are you genuinely interested in the other person in your interactions? Do you listen as much as you share?

BE DIFFERENT

- If you are looking to build a new relationship, select one or more techniques from the list of "Ten Ways to Find New Relationships" and proactively make a plan to get out there.
- When interacting with people on a daily basis, remember to ask questions about their day and their life, and try to be fully present (no phones, no distractions) when they answer.

CHAPTER 8

LEVEL III

THE FEMALE GROUP

The Four Levels of Relationship

Level I. My relationship with myself

Level II. My one-on-one relationships

Level III. My group (3 or more) relationships

Level IV. My relationships with everyone else

The third level of the Tribe is the group. Groups can be physical or virtual. The group is an elevated level of relationship that gives us exponential connection, particularly as we age. Imagine not one, but three, six, or even ten people who travel life's journey with us.

When I think back to my childhood, I was raised with a strong sense of personal value, and I had a few strong one-on-one relationships. I also created lots of groups for different purposes.

However, deep down, I still wanted to find a group of people I could enjoy life with. Groups are complementary to our one-on-one relationships and create another avenue to connect and build life-changing, supportive friendships. These connections allow us not only to feel fulfilled but to have a more significant personal and professional impact.

Groups can be found in some of the same places that we find our one-on-one friends. We can also form groups around causes, rituals, events, people, work, celebrations, and even pain. Group dynamics are also a little more complex to navigate, so having a Tribe mindset is really important for group success.

While writing this book, I spoke to numerous women about this concept of female groups. I began to notice a consistent pattern form in terms of the types of female groups that women gravitate toward. Additionally, as I reflected on my journey of Tribe, I also noticed not every group began the same way or had the same objective. Following extensive research, I concluded there are at least six types of female groups that one might encounter. Let's unpackage the findings.

THE RESEARCH

I have formed groups since I was about six years old. However, most of the groups were transient, and only one group has lasted nearly 20 years. As part of my research, I discovered I was not alone. Sixty-five percent of women who were a part of a group participated in three or more groups (see figure below).

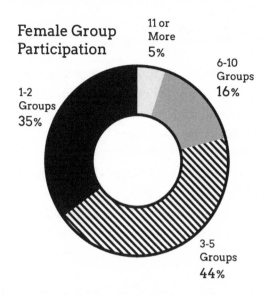

Female Group Participation

- 11 or More 5%
- 6-10 Groups 16%
- 1-2 Groups 35%
- 3-5 Groups 44%

WHAT ARE THESE GROUPS THAT HELP US FIND BELONGING?

In my research I have studied six different types of groups that women participate in (see figure below). Each of these groups impact our lives in different ways. Let's explore what they are, how they work, and the challenges that we may experience.

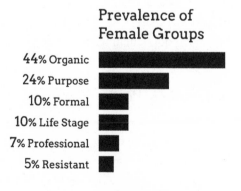

Prevalence of Female Groups

- 44% Organic
- 24% Purpose
- 10% Formal
- 10% Life Stage
- 7% Professional
- 5% Resistant

THE ORGANIC GROUP
What Is It and Why Does It Work?

The most common of all groups are organic groups. Organic groups form naturally. When speaking to a member of an organic group, you might often hear: "I can't recall when our relationship began; we just clicked."

Organic groups are typically childhood friends, girlfriends, and family members who have formed a special and unique bond. Organic groups happen without a lot of work, at least initially. The proximity or personalities of the group tend to make it easy and natural.

My very first group was organic. So much so that I can barely recall how it became a group. The first member was my best friend, and for the life of us we can't figure out to this day what was the catalyst that brought us together as friends. The two of us spent an inordinate amount of time together. Then I had another friend who shared a common interest with my best friend, and we invited her to hang out. The great thing about this particular group is we grew up together, attended the same high school, and had mutual friends. It was effortless. For several years we were inseparable. We organized lunches, movie nights, barbecues, spa visits, poetry parties, and more. We had a great time hanging out, laughing, and loving life.

What Challenges Might We Experience in Organic Groups?

Organic groups can be some of the most impactful Tribes in our lives. There's a lot of commonality and history that exists in organic groups. For this very reason, conversely, they can also be subject to controversies and challenges. When organic groups form, there are no guideposts or rules to direct the structure, which is both a blessing and a curse. You may also find that organic groups experience the hardest, most difficult splinters. These are the groups that were supposed to follow us for life, and when they don't work, the cuts are deep.

THE PURPOSE GROUP
What Is It and Why Does It Work?

If a person is goal-driven and likes to give time to a specific cause, community service, or nonprofit, a purpose group might be the correct fit. Coming in at number two in terms of prevalence, members of purpose groups like to get things done and tend to form around a specific purpose or activity. Examples of purpose groups include movements and causes. People who join these types of groups are very clear about what they want to accomplish.

Over the years, I have formed numerous purpose groups around health and wellness activities. One such group included friends who attended kickboxing classes regularly. Another group was for wives, spouses, and friends and involved connecting to exercise and holding each other accountable. I have helped to start a movement that focuses on spreading random acts of kindness. I am also several years into the creation of a kids' group that focuses on helping children acquire practical life and relationship skills to prepare them for the future while creating a safe place for belonging.

Some of my most impactful purpose groups to date are *Designed For Impact* (DFI) and *Young Original Unstoppable* (YOU). These purpose groups aim to connect women around topics they care about to inspire positive personal and professional change. You can learn more about DFI at www.iamdfi.com and YOU at www.youplusme.io.

What Challenges Might We Experience in Purpose Groups?

What I found with my purpose groups, and through interviews for this book, is that purpose groups can either have longevity or be transient. In order not to be disappointed, when joining a purpose group, appreciate and expect that the fluidity and commitment of the members may waiver over time. A purpose group may require more work than we bargained for to keep it together.

Over the years as I have created various groups, I have learned that purpose groups typically include volunteers and people who are passionate about the cause. However, even with sincere passion and the best intentions, life takes over. It's inevitable that from time to time, members simply can't commit in the way that they want to. When we are leading or a part of a purpose group, we have to prepare and plan for the ebb and flow of support. Don't be disheartened when people pull away. With strong planning and a Tribe mindset that says, "I will take whatever gift, talent, or time you can give to me," purpose groups can make a huge impact in the world.

THE FORMAL GROUP
What Is It and Why Does It Work?

If you like structure and rules, a life stage group may be what you are looking for. Tied at number three with life stage groups, a formal group comes together in very clear, organized, and structured ways. Typically, there are clear criteria for entry, operating rules, and a formal hierarchy for how decisions and activities are carried out. Examples of formal groups are trade or professional associations, sororities, and clubs. The interesting thing about the formal group is that other types of groups can also be formal. However, it's the rigid structure of the formal group that gives us pause to pull it out on its own.

What Challenges Might We Experience with a Formal Group?

When pressed for time and struggling to keep up with life, the rigidity of a formal group may present a challenge. It's important to understand the rules of the specific formal group up front when joining so as not to find yourself out of step with the group.

LIFE STAGE GROUPS
What Is It and Why Does It Work?

Tied with formal groups in terms of prevalence, life stage groups generally follow our life's journey. For example, these groups can start in childhood and pop up through college, when we marry, have kids, or retire. These are the groups that help us to navigate the stages of life, and if we are lucky, they can stay intact for a lifetime.

What Challenges Might We Experience in Life Stage Groups?

It would not be uncommon for a life stage group to disband as we move into the next stage of life. It is important to prepare ourselves mentally and emotionally for the possibility of loss when we or other members of the group move one. However, with intentional proactive conversation, it might be possible for the group to reset, instead of disbanding.

PROFESSIONAL GROUPS
What Is It and Why Does It Work?

Professional groups are groups that typically form around work-related interests and networks. These groups are not as prevalent as the other groups, coming in at number five. This type of group thrives on the exchange of ideas and information. The group may include people we work with today or have worked with in the past. Professional groups can also include people who come together from varying industries to share and network.

I have been part of a few professional groups over time. Recently, I was invited by a mentor to join an amazing professional group of women who want to help other women develop communication skills. This group is an excellent example of women coming together to fill a gap and help each other grow. I am honored to be a part of this group.

We know many of us find our relationships at work. In our day-to-day interactions, we might find that office hours are not enough and choose to spend time away from the office, enjoying each other's company. No matter the genesis of a professional group, it can be immensely helpful in providing support and navigating a career journey.

What Challenges Might We Experience in Professional Groups?

Many people try to keep their personal and professional lives separate, and sometimes it's for good reasons. When we mix business and pleasure, sometimes boundaries can get crossed, which creates conflicts. For example, we have found a group at work and we really click. As a result, we fall into the trap of talking about people and confidential workplace subjects, while in social settings. The reverse may be true, too. We might find ourselves in a situation where, because of our group relationship, we possess confidential information about a person (e.g., clinical depression, a family crisis) that should be escalated at work, but we're afraid to do that. Addressing the issue from a professional perspective might be delicate and could compromise the group if not handled carefully.

THE RESISTANT GROUP
What Is It and Why Does It Work?

Last, and thankfully so, are the resistant groups. Resistant groups are the groups that we would typically never choose to be a part of. These are groups formed in the face of crisis or adversity. They can take many forms, but some of the most common resistant groups are formed because of shared painful experiences such as divorce, loss of a loved one, or illness. We never set out to become part of this type of group, but when we find these peers, they can be life-saving. These groups often create unbreakable bonds that can last for a lifetime or a critical season.

While I was writing this book, I spoke to a friend who had recently divorced. She said to me: "Leah, I never intended to need a group to cope with divorce, but I am so thankful to have this group of women to help me navigate the journey."

What Challenges Might You Experience in Resistant Groups?

Resistant groups are amazing because they connect us with people who understand our pain. However, they can also be a reminder of the pain as time passes. Perhaps we have healed and are ready to move on, but the other members in the group are still struggling. We might want to pull away so we can continue our healing. As a result, we may experience a sense of guilt because it is time for us to move on.

THE GOAL IS TO UNDERSTAND, NOT TO COMPLICATE

We could look at this data and say: "Ugh, that's so formal and complicated. Why do we need to put the groups we form into categories or boxes?"

I encourage pushing that thought aside and thinking of the explanation of these six groups as a new language to describe and understand our group Tribes. Each group has its benefits, pitfalls, and challenges. The idea is to leverage the data to help us understand the groups we form and participate in. With this deeper understanding, the goal is to skip some of the group challenges that get in the way.

The good news is, based on the data, if we choose to look for a group, chances are we may find a group for the long haul. The data shows that 80 percent of women belonged to a group for three or more years, with more than 55 percent participating in a group for six years or more.

Female Group Participation Duration

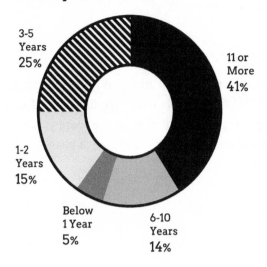

3-5 Years 25%

11 or More 41%

1-2 Years 15%

Below 1 Year 5%

6-10 Years 14%

REMEMBER

There are different types of groups we can join or form. Each group has its benefits and challenges to consider before we dive in.

Groups don't work for everyone and can be complicated to navigate, but when we find the right groups, the data proves we can stick with them. If you have never experienced a group before, perhaps it's something to consider.

REFLECT

- How many groups have you participated in throughout your life? List one to three of them and name as many members as you can. How long have you been a member of each group?

- How has each group added to your life? What challenges have you faced and why?

BE DIFFERENT

Think about the group you are a part of or potentially want to start or join. With a deeper understanding of the dynamics and challenges of groups, how can you prepare yourself or your groups to be more resilient in the face of change?

CHAPTER 9

LEVEL IV

OPENNESS OPENS DOORS

The Four Levels of Relationship

> Level I. My relationship with myself

> Level II. My one-on-one relationships

> Level III. My group (3 or more) relationships

> Level IV. My relationships with everyone else

The fourth and final level of relationship is the way we connect and relate to everyone else who comes into our sphere of influence. These connections can be fleeting, recurring, or transition into long-lasting connections or friendships. The questions become:

If we have one-on-one and group relationships, how do we handle everyone else?

How much capacity do we have to share our lives with others?

DON'T SHUT THE DOOR

Having intentional Level IV relationships was another one of my big aha moments. Often when we find a happy relationship, we might tend to relax into it and ignore the rest of the world. Not because we intend to be unkind, but because we are enjoying the belonging and investing in the relationships that we have found. Such was the case for me.

I discovered that the sense of security and safety I found in my nearly twenty-year Tribe had led me to close off a part of myself to the rest of the world. With a busy job, two young kids, a husband, and an active social life with my Tribe, I felt my relationship slate was full. As a result, I did little to cultivate some of the relationships I developed in the past, and I was not open to finding new ones. I don't recall intentionally being unkind to anyone, but I know I did not go out of my way to add to my Tribe. I had arrived. I was safe.

If I think back, my Level IV mind shift began when I moved into my first executive role. Many of my connections were not experientially equipped to help me navigate the challenges with moving into a new level of leadership. Executive positions are often isolating, especially for human resource executives. As an HR professional, you constantly have to straddle the delicate balance between acting in the interest of the company and advocating for employees. I was lonely and, at times, felt as if I had nowhere to turn. I had not spent enough time cultivating some of my past relationships due to a heavy work schedule. In my guilt, I decided my best bet was simply to figure it out and navigate this new part of my career on my own.

It was around the same time I met a woman as a result of a professional referral. She was vibrant, loved life, had an easy way with people, and took a deep personal interest in my life. To be honest, I was a bit skeptical at first. Was the interest purely professional, or was she interested in me as a person? There was a part of me that remained closed-off because I was safe and not "accepting" any new close friends.

As the years passed by, I did not take down my invisible wall, and eventually, guilt began to set in because of my value of trust. The reality is, I knew I had not allowed myself to fully trust her. It wasn't because she did not deserve my trust, but because I had decided that my relationship slate was full.

I had to do some work on me, and in the exploration, I realized my hesitation was not about her. My reticence was about my past experiences with women. I had subconsciously decided I didn't want to let anyone else in at this stage in my life. As I reflected on the situation, I found it was unfair to her. My lack of openness was not a factor of time or any other reason. I had just closed myself off. With a clear picture that my behavior was out of alignment with my values, I decided to be open. I decided to allow the pattern of our relationship to guide me, not some deep-seated negative past experience.

With intentional focus, I shifted my mindset to be more open to all of the amazing people and women who naturally crossed my path. *Designed for Impact* catapulted me into a world where meeting new people was par for the course. With a newfound resolve to be more open, I began to connect with people more often.

As I began to shift my mindset, I found I did have time. Now don't misunderstand me—we only have so much time in the day. Time constraints won't allow us to go deep with every single person we meet. However, we can be kind, engage in the moment, genuinely ask how someone is doing, and then stop to listen to the answer.

The realization that I could leverage my sense of value and my belonging to simply be open to the world with no fear was freeing. When I projected that openness to all of the people whom I met, they were happy to share and project that same openness back at me.

REAL QUEENS FIX EACH OTHER'S CROWNS

As we begin to take on a Tribe mindset and unlock the formula of Believe + Belong = Be Different, we have an incredible opportunity to look for ways to encourage and support women and girls. For me, some days it could be a simple, "You look great today!" On other occasions, it could mean taking someone to lunch or sending a quick encouraging text. It costs me nothing other than a few words or minutes. The opportunity for me to give and make someone's day is priceless.

As I began to apply this new Level IV mindset intentionally, relationships were mended, and new personal and professional connections were made. I felt happier and more fulfilled. The world was a much better place. At this level, we don't have to fear rejection because we have belonging within ourselves and in the relationships we have chosen. By taking down our walls, we open ourselves up to being kinder, more productive citizens in the world. The great thing about Level IV is that if new relationships don't play out as we hoped, we know we will survive. We still have personal value and belonging. Isn't this a much better way to live?

REMEMBER

Life becomes richer when we intentionally leverage the safety of our belonging to be more open with everyone else. Our human capacity and fear can get in the way, but when we are intentional about our relationships, we can find and thrive with our Tribes.

REFLECT

- Are you operating with a Level IV mindset, or do you need to make a conscious shift? If not, what might you be protecting yourself from? How can you begin to shift your mindset?
- Be on the lookout for how you might notice and comment on another woman's "crown." Once your action is taken, note how they responded and how you felt about the interaction.

BE DIFFERENT

- Having identified the places you find belonging, identify two or three relationships or situations where you can test your new Level IV mindset.
- When you are out and about, talk to strangers; say "thank you" and "good morning," tell the woman next to you her outfit is fabulous, tell a friend or coworker what you love about them. Take note of the impact you have on them and how it makes you feel.

CHAPTER 10

NAVIGATING THE LEVELS OF RELATIONSHIP

I spoke at an event about the importance of being open and different in our relationships. A few weeks after the event, I was talking to a girlfriend, and she said, "Leah, I am right there with you when you talk about believing in my value and finding belonging. However, when you get to Be Different, the Level IV part of the equation, I just lose you. I hate meeting new people. It's nerve-wracking, and I just find it difficult."

Having felt that way from time to time myself, I had to take a step back and think about what I was asking people to do. Was I saying to abandon the fear of rejection, and put yourself out there anyway?

Well, yes and no. When I followed up with my friend to collect more information about her thoughts, I realized the reason she was struggling with Be Different was because of fear and trust.

Here is the thing, and this is one of the critical pillars on which Tribes are built: there ought to be requirements for how deeply we allow people to access our lives! Just because we choose to be open to new relationships does not mean that everyone should access our lives and hearts in the same way.

WHAT IS A RELATIONSHIP?

As I contemplated the thought about how deeply we allow people into our lives, I had another critical aha. When we enter into a relationship with someone, particularly as women, we want people whom we can trust and connect with. However, as we have learned, there are different levels of relationships and depth. Not attending to both can sometimes get us into trouble.

There is a body of research by Robert Dunbar that found the average number of intimate relationships we can sustain in any meaningful way is around five. It further revealed that we can typically manage about 15 good friends, 50 friends, 150 meaningful contacts, 500 acquaintances, and 1,500 people we recognize.[28] If we only have the mental and emotional capacity for five close friends, fifteen good friends, and fifty friends, what do we do about the potentially hundreds of people we meet?

First, let's define a relationship. Relationship is how two things are connected or a state of being related or interrelated.[29] We can easily infer from this definition that not all relationships are connected in the same way. Practically, if we want a specific type of relationship, like friendship, marriage, or a best friend, we have to behave in a way that will change the nature of the relationship. In some ways, choosing a relationship is a three-step process.

- Step 1: Be open and choose how to behave toward someone.
- Step 2: Decide the depth or type of relationship we want.

- Step 3. Do the work; invest the time, effort, and emotion needed to deepen a relationship.

The problem that surfaces in society today is we "friend" people on social media, which implies a depth to the relationship that is inaccurate and inappropriate. Then we look to add depth when the relationship-building process is actually the other way around.

THE PARADOX OF OPENNESS AND CAPACITY

As an advocate of Level IV openness, for me, this idea that we only have so much capacity was a big problem. How can we be open if we only have a limited ability to absorb relationships?

It was in exploring this paradox of openness and capacity that I realized a big part of becoming more open meant I also had to be authentic and realistic about my relationship capacity. Whenever I meet someone, I have to choose how I want to "behave" toward them or treat them in the moment—that's openness. However, if I want the relationship to be more profound, more than just a simple hello, I have to invest time, effort, and emotion to create relationship depth.

For example, for many years, I believed that to be authentic, I had to connect with a person on an in-depth individual level. However, as someone who travels and connects with lots of people, I found this to be not only very difficult, but impossible! I will never forget that during a two-month conference season, I made a list of everyone to whom I had said: "We should connect."

When I added it up, the list totaled more than sixty people. As

I tried to make my way through my "coffee date" list, it became painfully evident that I did not have the time, and ultimately I failed.

It was after this failure that I realized I could be open and choose how to "behave" toward someone when I met them. However, I also had to understand that there are only so many hours in the day. I had to be realistic about my capacity. Some days, even if I wanted more, to be my most authentic self, I had to appreciate people where I met them and then leave them there.

Realizing that I could authentically have relationships without depth was a freeing moment for me. It's one of many Tribe mindset shifts I discovered. I was able to put aside my guilt and simply enjoy the person and the occasion. My decision to be different, more open, created the opportunity for a deeper relationship, but in the first instance, merely connecting and being more open in the moment was enough.

Here are two principles to help us manage this paradox of openness and capacity.

1. **While we can be open, we should have criteria for how deeply we allow someone to access our lives.** I have a few criteria that work well for me to go deeper into a relationship with someone. We both have to:
   A. Have common beliefs and values.
   B. Be willing to invest time, effort, and emotion in the relationship.
   C. Give of ourselves for the benefit of the other.
   D. Demonstrate that we are trustworthy through our actions.

2. **Be clear and realistic about our relationship capacity.** This clarity will allow us to navigate our relationships with greater authenticity, enjoying them at whatever stage or depth we choose. Choosing to define the level of investment we want to make in a person or Tribe is a critical step. People can become disillusioned if we are not genuine with our intentions.

I remember going to a conference and talking to a woman about mentoring. She told me about her struggles to find new relationships and support from women because of what appeared as a lack of genuineness. Often, she would attend an event, meet an impressive woman, and exchange contact details. Then when she followed up, the contact would fail to respond, leaving her feeling blown off, rejected, and disappointed. I have been guilty of that in the past, wanting to be supportive, but not having the time.

So as not to frustrate or leave the impression we don't care, it's crucial to define and set parameters. If we simply don't have the bandwidth, say that.

I told the young woman not to lose hope, but to continue to reach out and try to expand her Tribe. However, I told her that if she was feeling blown off, that it was perfectly okay to say, "Hey, I notice you seem busy. If it's not a good time or you do not have the capacity right now, I understand."

Ladies, we must be thoughtful on both sides of the relationship equation. Silence does not mean rejection, but we need to be crystal clear with people about the capacity that we have to engage. The goal is to communicate our capacity so we can connect with people authentically and realistically.

If we are on the receiving end of a "No, I don't have capacity," while we may be disappointed, we should not become disillusioned. There are people out there who need us. Every relationship is not the right fit, and that is okay. Connections can also be situational. Sometimes we might find that we are at our max capacity, but the opportunity for a deeper relationship with someone is so compelling that we consciously make space for them in our lives. That is great! We just have to consider and manage the impact of running above capacity.

In summary, always remember that our lack of ability to go deep with everyone that we meet does not make us less genuine. It's just a reality of our human capacity. When we remain open in our initial interactions and communicate about our capacity, we can navigate this paradox with clarity and authenticity.

WHEN OPENNESS SCARES US

While writing this chapter, I googled, what is the greatest fear we have as humans? The number-one return on that day was: The fear of failure is the greatest fear humans have. Every other fear is simply an avatar of the fear of failure.

Whenever we open ourselves up to a relationship, there's the possibility that we might fail in our openness and experience rejection. For some of us, we can double down and talk ourselves into trying, and for others, that fear physically paralyzes us and keeps us from moving forward.

THE PSYCHOLOGY OF FEAR

When we consider the psychology behind fear, it is both biochemical and emotional, and one of the most intense emotions we have.

On a biochemical level, when we feel there's a threat of any sort, our brains and bodies prepare for combat, and we can experience physical reactions: sweating, increased heart rate, high adrenaline. This reaction is known as the flight-or-fight reaction, which keeps us alert and prepares us to fight or run away.[30]

On an emotional level, our response to fear is unique to each of us. Some of us are fear-junkies. The experiences that would bring some of us joy bring deep fear to others. For example, my husband loves roller coasters, jumping out of planes, and spontaneous travel. I, on the other hand, prefer to keep my feet on the ground and plan my vacations.

Fear shows up in our relationships in a very similar way. Some of us are excited about the idea of new relationships, while others experience physical and emotional reactions that make us want to run. Wanting to understand more, I spoke with a friend who struggles with the fear of rejection.

What was fascinating about our conversation is that she remembered a point in her life, when she did not fear rejection and was more open. However, along the way, she experienced harsh judgment in her relationships, which created a deep fear of rejection. Her fears continued to evolve to the point that if someone disliked a gift she might give them out of the kindness of her heart, like a pot of soup, she internalized that dislike as a rejection of herself.

Wanting to understand this idea of relationship fear more

deeply, I spoke to clinical psychologist Dr. Kelly Holder, and she shared:

"For most of us, fear, like all the rest of our negative emotions, is often avoided at all costs. This fear is not just in our minds. The fear comes from either observed or lived experiences, and can cause us to see relationships as unsafe."

Dr. Holder went on to say, "For some of us, this makes the idea of being a member of a Tribe feel almost impossible. These negative experiences wire us to operate on the premise that we do not belong, and maybe we are not capable of belonging. With these mindsets on board, we can kiss the notion of being different and being open to new relationships and experiences good-bye."

CONQUERING FEARS

There are several ways to address our fears. One of the ways is through exposure. When we repeatedly expose ourselves to situations in controlled ways (systematic desensitization) or in significant quantities (flooding), we become more familiar and reduce our fear response.[31]

If you struggle with fear in your relationships, perhaps Dr. Holder's words and these tactics can give you some hope. Fear is a natural human reaction, and we have options on how to tackle it! Here are a few practical suggestions that we can use to move away from our fear of relationships to become more open.

1. **Start from a place of comfort**. When engaging with new people, we can do it around something that we love: a hobby, passion, or interest. When we are participating in something

that we love, such as cooking or eating out, we have a more natural tendency to be confident and ease into conversations because we are comfortable in our passion.

2. **Find a (buddy) buffer.** When venturing into new relationship situations, recruit a family member or friend to come along. Sometimes just having someone there for moral support can boost our confidence and give us the time and space that we need to feel safe in the relationship.

3. **Prepare and be inquisitive.** Earlier in the book, I talked about being curious when we engage in new relationships. To help ease the anxiety of the initial interaction, prepare a few questions ahead of time. Asking questions can reduce some of the intensity of that initial interaction and give us time to relax and, hopefully, allow us to find things in common.

4. **Go where the warmth is.** Some people are naturally friendly and make us feel comfortable. When venturing out, find the people who intuitively feel safe to you, and engage with them first. Additionally, think about your body language; are you projecting openness, warmth, or fear? Try to breathe, relax, and be open.

5. **Be patient and get help if needed.** There are different ways to deal with fear, and some of them take repetition and time. The key is to be intentional about finding ways to get out there and expose yourself to new people in a way that feels safe for you. If the idea of meeting new people is too overwhelming, you may also want to consider getting help so you can better understand the root of your fear and then move forward.

According to Dr. Holder, "If we have experienced trauma, abuse, and toxic relationships, seeking help is paramount. Help can take the form of individual therapy or group treatment, which is a powerful option for many. Skills I find highly beneficial for improving our ability to believe and belong are addressed in a course of treatment called Dialectical Behavior Therapy. The skills include mindfulness, interpersonal effectiveness, emotional regulation, and distress tolerance."

REMEMBER

Navigating relationships can be complicated. Even when we want to be open, we only have so much capacity (time, effort, emotion), and that is okay. When we communicate our capacity, we can navigate relationships with authenticity.

New connections can also evoke fear, which is a natural response. We have tools at our disposal to manage our concerns. With effort and, if needed, a little help, we can navigate our way to openness and find connection.

REFLECT

- Think of a time when you wanted a deeper relationship with someone, but either they or you did not have the time to engage deeply. How did you feel about it? Do you still wish you could engage with that person? Have you had a conversation to figure out if there's a level of engagement that might work for both of you?
- Do you struggle with relationship fear? Are you kind to yourself as you navigate your issues of fear, or do you perpetuate a feeling of failure? What actions can you take, or what support do you need to conquer your relationship fears?

BE DIFFERENT

- As you meet new people, try to be more open and allow yourself to enjoy the moment. Be present. It could lead to a lifelong connection, or it might be fleeting. Either scenario is okay.
- As you engage in your relationships, be mindful of the type of connection and the depth you want. Is there a boundary you need to set for yourself or communicate to the other party?
- If needed, explore the reasons for your relationship fear. Proactively seek the help and support you need so that, day by day, you are conquering your fears, finding your Tribe, and deepening your relationships.

CHAPTER 11

MOVEMENT INSPIRES MOVEMENT

A TRIBE STORY

 My name is Ingrid. I have lived my life across all of the levels of Tribe—from learning to love myself as a child to finding positive one-on-one relationships and a group who supports me no matter what. Yes, there were hard times and difficult lessons, but there was also joy, connection, and incredible friendships. This is my *Assemble the Tribe* story.

The first positive female relationships I observed were my mom and her sisters. When I was a child, they spent time together regularly; for my mom, that was her Tribe. They cooked, cleaned, watched each other's children, and knew how to party together, too. These examples of the bond of real friendship had a stabilizing impact on me. I knew what good relationships looked like, and I wanted these in my life.

LEVEL I—BELIEVING IN ME

As a little girl, I loved who I was. Even though people were not always kind, I remember looking in the mirror and saying, "You're not ugly! You're a nice person! You're a really good friend."

I felt a sense of value from a young age. When I think back, part of the reason was because of my aunt and her friend. I loved visiting my aunt, who lived next door to my grandmother. It was my favorite place in the world to visit. My aunt ran a guest-house and entertained a lot. What I remember the most is she treated me like everything I thought and felt mattered. When I was with her I felt heard, respected, safe, and loved.

There were always lots of interesting people around, locals and visitors alike. There was one regular visitor whom I will never forget. Mrs. W was tall, classy, elegant, and always beautifully dressed. Whenever she was visiting from the United States, Mrs. W would find me and look me in the eyes. She would say, "You are so beautiful. Your neck is so long you look like an Egyptian queen."

Even though I was a little girl, Mrs. W made me feel beautiful. She and my aunt would invite me to afternoon tea just to talk. They became my first Tribe. Their kind words and attention had a tremendous impact on me.

As a child, life can seem effortless, but as we age, it's easy to fall into the traps of doubting our value and comparing ourselves to others. There are people who we may feel are more intelligent, more beautiful, just more than we are. There may be people who try to pull us down to build themselves up, but we can't listen to those voices, and I didn't.

As I aged, some days it was a struggle to remember who I was and that I was valuable, but I did. I remember having self-chats, "You're more! You have worth! You're very creative! You're beautiful."

LEVEL II—MY ONE-ON-ONE FRIENDS

I am grateful to have a few good sister friends. These friends we might not see often. It does not matter if we see them every week or every three years; we just pick up where we left off. I have a few friends like this; we grew up together, and to this day, we are there for each other, we encourage each other, and over the years this has not changed.

Not every relationship I had was comfortable. I remember in college there was a friend—well, I thought she was my friend. We used to do everything together, but over time I started to see a change in her. When we were out with friends, perhaps at dinner, she would try to pull me down to build herself up. To this day, I don't understand why she did it because she was beautiful, intelligent, and talented.

When I think back, one of the real issues was that her belief system was different than mine. There were things she wanted to do that I didn't believe in. Thankfully my sense of self-worth was strong enough that I told her no. In the end, we simply grew apart.

Sometimes relationships work, and others we have to walk away from. The key is to know when to lean in and when to walk away.

LEVEL III—MY GROUP, MY SISTER TRIBE

Fast-forward. Life was speeding along. I got married, and in addition to my teenage daughter, I had a little girl and boy under the age of five. My life revolved around the children. With the pace of life and the demands of family, I did not see my one-on-one friends very often. I was lonely. At one point, I remember crying and praying, "I need some friends who are going to love me and encourage me." Unbeknownst to me, my eldest daughter was praying that I would find friends, too.

One day out of the blue, a cousin called and asked me to join a group of married women who got together once a month. I remember the first meeting. I was a little bit shy, but after that first get-together, I knew the group was just what the doctor ordered. It was the perfect place for me.

Over the years that Tribe has been there. If I was going through issues with my children or work challenges, they showed up. Encouragement to exercise. Encouragement to cook and experiment with new recipes. Support to pursue my passions. At least once a week, somebody from my Tribe called to encourage me.

Recently, I decided to make a significant life change. I have always been creative, and art has always been a part of my life. I create something beautiful out of discarded materials. My Tribe supported me when I decided to focus on my art. Whenever I showed a piece, they affirmed me, which made me want to delve into it even more. They made me want to do my best. After spending time with them, I would go home and say, "You know what? This art thing could be something massive."

I am thankful for the fateful day when I received the invitation to join my group Tribe. I learned what it means to accept people for who they are and to want to be the best version of myself.

LEVEL IV—JUST BE OPEN

Sometimes when we have negative experiences with people, we become closed off. However, for me, it was never like that. I have my Tribes, and I hold them close to my heart; they remind me that it's safe to be open. I love meeting new people. They have unique ways of thinking and new ideas. Some people are afraid of being open, but to that I say, it does not have to be as hard as you think.

Sometimes openness can start with a kind word, and sometimes we don't even have to open our mouth, but just smile. The smile has to be a real smile, not a fake smile, and it can open the door for conversation and connection. A lot of people are looking for someone to simply care, and some days a smile or kind word is just the thing needed.

MY TOP FIVE

In summary, I believe I have lived a life of Tribe at every level. It hasn't always been easy, but I am grateful for the journey. As women, we must support each other and teach our daughters and our sons to do the same.

Here are my Top Five Ways to Be Different:

1. **Change Your Way of Thinking and Speaking:** The other day, I was with a young woman who started to talk about another woman. I said, "Wait a minute, now, that's not funny. It is very painful." We have to think of women as fellow sisters

and think differently, speak differently, about each other. Even in the moments that seem not to matter, we should build up other women.

2. **Speak to Yourself:** I know it sounds crazy, but regularly look in the mirror and encourage yourself, "You got this. You can do this." Believe in yourself and remind yourself of your value. Never stop pushing for your dreams.

3. **Be Kind to Other Women:** Being kind is easy. Thinking kindly and expecting the best helps people and our communities be better. Often we might wonder why people show up the way they do. There could be catastrophic things going on in their lives. When we are kind, we can make a difference in someone's life. I am always looking for cues: "What can I do? How can I be there for you? What's going on?

4. **Be Authentically You:** If we're not authentically ourselves, we can't touch lives in the way we are supposed to. I am an artist. That's how I share my passion with the world. Dozens of people have said, "Don't stop putting your work out there. It's very encouraging." Nine times out of ten, my art starts conversations and opens the door to talk about family, life, and beliefs.

5. **Movement Inspires Movement:** This is the tagline I use in my art. Think of a ball. When we push it, it picks up momentum and begins to move on its own. This idea of building our Tribes is no different. When we choose to change our ways of thinking, and pour into the life of a woman or little girl, as my aunt and her friend poured into me, we impact lives. Our actions will build momentum and change the world.

PART 3

Be Different (Living Life with Your Tribe)

CHAPTER 12

TAKE THE DARE

Finding relationships, particularly with women, can be complicated and daunting. The good news is, the steps to creating relationships tend to be the same. What makes the difference in how deep our relationship can go is the level of investment (time, effort, emotion) we are willing to make. When we are busy and worn out, sometimes it's challenging to figure out where to start.

Women tend to be givers and often struggle to prioritize life—work, family, self-care, and time with our Tribes. As a result, when we carve out a few precious moments to connect, we want it to be pleasant and fulfilling, not full of drama and discontent. That, combined with the complexity of history, biology, and social wiring makes the female relationship complicated!

Relationships are about choosing to invest and come together. However, I have learned over the years it's not just about getting together to hang out, the process of how we enter into our relationships matters as well.

When I formed my first group Tribe many years ago, I unknowingly followed four steps to create the group. While the steps work well in groups, we can also tick through them when we are connecting with people one-on-one. Checking through the steps can be a formal sit-down or a quick mental exercise. The way we do it doesn't really matter. The important thing is to create clarity so our relationships can thrive. There are four simple steps to the process:

I DARE you to follow these four simple steps or at least give them a try. As I walk you through the steps, I will use one of my group Tribes as an example to illustrate how each step can come to life.

STEP 1: DEFINE THE RELATIONSHIP

The original purpose of my group Tribe was to figure out how to master that thing called marriage. At the age of twenty-three, what did I know about being a wife? As the months passed by, life was good, but I knew I was a marital novice. I shared my instincts with a girlfriend, who tied the knot two months after me. She was feeling the same way. After talking about it for a while, we decided to create a group. It was to be a purpose group that would meet once a month—a book club to help us navigate the waters of marriage.

If we want to have healthy, sustaining Tribes, the first step is to define our relationships. Consider the following questions:

- What is the reason for this relationship?
- What type of interaction frequency do I/we want?
- For groups, how will people be invited or join? How will late joiners be added?
- How will we communicate (in person, virtually, etc.)?
- For groups, what type of group will it be?

When we create definition in our relationships, we create a path to clarify the support needed, and we can reduce conflict and stress.

Reminder: Step 1. Define the type of relationship. Be sure to focus on what it is and what it is not.

STEP 2: ACTIVATE TO STAY CONNECTED

An activator makes things happen. An activator is the person or persons who start a relationship, or they may be the catalyst who gets things going and then shifts out of the activator seat. The activator role can be assumed, assigned, or shared. Still, it's a critical role for long-term relationship success, particularly within groups.

In my group Tribe, the years passed by, and we routinely got together month after month laughing, talking, and sharing. Our get-togethers were over-the-top special and would typically include fine china, candles, and great food. Our mantra was that ladies' night was our time to pamper ourselves, and it should feel special. Month after month I would host. I enjoyed every moment of it, and on a few occasions, we even saw the sunrise.

Around year five, a few of us decided it was time to start families, and three newborns entered. Kids dramatically shifted the dynamics of our group, and it was a seismic shift for me. The new moms no longer wanted to hang out late, and my enthusiasm for hosting and organizing shifted from a 10: I can't wait, to about a 2: Do I have to? At this point, I no longer wanted to activate, so I put together a schedule for the group. Each of us would organize two months a year so no one person would feel the weight of activating all the time. I thought my plan was brilliant, except I often found myself reminding the organizer it was her turn. That reminder expanded to assisting with planning, and before too long, I was activating again, this time with two kids in tow.

I became very frustrated and would love to say I communicated effectively to the group, but I did not. Instead, with some resentment, I decided to suck it up and continue to activate because that was better than the alternative: not connecting.

The activator role does not just apply to groups. I was coaching a friend while writing this book, and she lamented about another friend who she believed did not care about their relationship. I asked her to tell me more. She said, "I am the one always reaching out. I am the one who always plans and makes an effort."

With exasperation, she said she was almost ready to give up. As we talked through her issues, we explored the differences in how people express love and their strengths. In the end, we concluded that her friend did love her, but she did not love by organizing their get-togethers; that was not her strength.

We all have natural gifts, and if activation is one, we should consider if we can activate without frustration because that's a valuable contribution we can bring to a relationship(s). If it's a group Tribe, you may need to organize or recruit others to help. Our lives are so busy and complicated that sometimes we need that one person who will say, "Stop, it's been too long—let's do this!"

I believe this idea of activation is particularly essential for women who are looking for sponsorship or mentorship. When we meet a woman who we think can play that role in our Tribe, she is likely professionally accomplished, impressive, and BUSY! If we want the relationship, it's our role as the mentee to activate.

For example, I have come across many women who have said, "Well, I have a mentor, but she never checks in or makes time for me."

In response I asked, "Do you follow up and persist with tracking her down?"

They answer, "Well, I tried, but I figure if she was invested in the relationship, she would make time."

In most instances where this conversation occurs, the mentee feels let down. Practically this way of thinking is a little naive.

Our sponsors and mentors are often pressed for time and need us to activate so they can add value to our lives.

I have three amazing female mentors. One is the CEO of her own company, and the remaining two women are senior executives who retired to sit on corporate boards. They have been busy from the first day I laid eyes on them. However, once they extended to me the opportunity to connect, I made it my role to activate. Even to this day, I check in on them via email. If I don't hear from them for a while, that's perfectly okay. I simply call their assistants and make an appointment or track them down. In some instances, I will drive to their homes to meet them or pick them up. I never have and never will expect them to do the work. The thing is, I activated, and over the years, we have all benefited greatly. I have been able to grow and develop because of their investment in me, and they have been able to give back, mold, and impact a life. As I have matured, our relationships have come full circle, and I can also help them as well.

Reminder: Step 2. Activate to stay connected, and in the case of groups, recruit others to help.

STEP 3: REACH OUT AND INVITE CONNECTION

Back to the group story, once we decided on the purpose of the group and who the initial activators were, it was time to reach out and invite other people to connect. Sometimes it happens organically, and sometimes it is a structured process. In my case, with my group Tribe, my friend and I spent hours thinking about who we would invite and why, the books we'd read, and where we would get together. Having had several painful experiences in the past, I even sent up a few prayers that we would get it right! In the end, we settled on several married women whom we either individually or collectively knew well and made the calls. To our surprise, every single woman (except for one—we will come back to this) said yes without hesitation.

I was too young to notice or even appreciate it at the time, but most women are open to connection. However, most of us don't know where to start. I remember reaching out to one person in particular. When I told her about the group, she broke down in tears, exclaiming that my call was an answer to her prayers! In fact, many years later, her adult daughter said to me, "Thank you for inviting my mom to your group; she was so lonely, and your invitation changed her life."

The female group data backs up this perspective as well. At some point in our lives, just over half of us (55 percent) have been asked to join a group, while 29 percent of us have tried to find a group. When I questioned, What was the impact of being asked?

- 59 percent of women who were asked to join a group were interested.
- 26 percent were wary, but still curious.

Based on the research, we can conclude that most women, if asked, would be interested in exploring new relationships.

There is one crucial point to note about reaching out. Remember when we made the calls to ask the women to join the group? One woman said no. It just so happened that she did not enjoy reading books. If we are asked or want to enter into a one-on-one or group relationship, but it's not the right fit, that's okay! Think about the impact if we allow ourselves to enter into relationships with the wrong person or group! It's better to say no than to travel down a path that will likely end in disappointment for you or the other party.

Taking the time to reach out, invite, and bring people together is a critical step in the process. An idea is just an idea without action to bring it to life. One of the greatest gifts we can give to another human being is to reach out and say, "You matter. I want to get to know you better."

Reminder: Step 3. To build or expand our Tribes, we have to reach out and invite connection.

STEP 4: EXAMINE INDIVIDUAL MOTIVATIONS

When we started the book club, we did not examine individual motivations. I figured it was not needed because it was a group with a clear purpose. However, I have found that personal motivations for entering into a Tribe often extend beyond the purpose of the group. Out of interest, I recently asked the group about their motivations for joining the group. To my surprise, I heard three or four different versions of why we started. Examining the motivations is an important—no, critical—step.

Even if we have defined the purpose of our relationship, it's always beneficial to have a more in-depth conversation. When forming a new relationship, we bring our shared goals and interests. We also bring our beliefs, values, experiences, pains, upbringings, and scars. If we want successful long-term relationships, examining the individual needs is important. Consider answers to the following questions:

- What is my motivation for seeking this relationship?
- What benefit will the relationship bring to each party?

In my case, our group evolved without a lot of formal conversation. However, over the years, there were some hiccups along the way: organizing get-togethers, personality styles, maturity, and how we spent our time together. These were minor kinks that could have been resolved with up-front conversations or intentional discussions along the way.

You might be thinking, "I have been down this road before and was burned. I can't trust women."

Don't give up yet! Remember, we are not investing in relationships just for relationships' sake; we need them so we can survive and live our best, healthiest, and longest lives. Relationships don't happen overnight. They require investments of our time, effort, and, most critically, our emotions. It takes some work, but when we get it right, the impact is life-altering.

Reminder: Step 4: Examine individual motivations before you get going with your Tribe.

One final point: we won't necessarily complete all of the steps at once or in order. Sometimes we need time to bring clarity. I remember on one occasion a woman reached out to me. We had a great meeting. We talked about our beliefs and values and how we could potentially support each other, but neither of us were crystal clear on how the relationship would evolve. I remember walking away from that initial meeting not really knowing what to do with the relationship. Over time, as we continued to connect, the reason for our relationship became clearer.

TIP: For relationship clarity, take the DARE, and if needed, give yourself time.

REMEMBER

Every relationship needs clarity. When we DARE ourselves to take the time to examine why our relationships are important and understand how they can add value to our lives, we open ourselves up to thrive.

REFLECT

- Have you ever been in a relationship where the purpose was not clearly defined? How did that lack of definition impact the relationship?
- If you are an activator, in what Tribes do you play this role? Do you want to be in this activator role? If so, how does that serve you and the group positively? If you don't want the responsibilities of the activator, what do you need to do to remove yourself from this role?
- If you are part of a group Tribe, is there a written or unwritten rule about how people can join your Tribe? Does everyone understand the process?

BE DIFFERENT

- When forming relationships, take the DARE together or, at a minimum, check the steps for yourself. Consider discussing the steps with the other individual(s) to ensure clarity as you move forward.
- If you are an activator, ensure that you have capacity to activate. If you have limited time, ask for help. Don't be an activator hog. Sometimes it's good to let others take a turn to keep the Tribe connecting.

CHAPTER 13

ENJOYING THE FLOW

When we experience relationship success, there's often a flow, a natural rhythm of sorts. Based on my research and experience, there are a few factors and steps we can take to keep our Tribes healthy. Let's explore them together.

WHAT DRIVES TRIBE SUCCESS?

Based on my study, there are four drivers that contribute to the Tribe success of female groups (see graphic below). While the model is derived from my analysis of group relationships, in practice, it can apply to our one-on-one relationships as well. I call it the Tribe Success Model:

Tribe Success Model

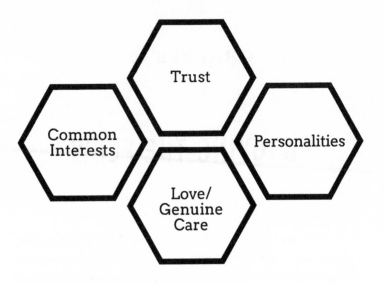

COMMON INTERESTS

No surprise, the number-one contributor to Tribe success was common interests. For most of us, our lives, to a large extent, are driven by our responsibilities to family and career. So much so that when we have downtime, we have a natural tendency to want to explore hobbies, passions, and interests that connect us with people who share the same needs. When we intentionally find people who share our interests, we can quickly create a strong foundation for a successful relationship.

Conversely, when common interest or purpose are not aligned, we may experience friction. I remember on one occasion I asked a friend to join a group I had set up. After about a year, it became clear that it was not working for her or the group. Had we taken the time to examine her motivations up front, we could have saved her and the group a few difficult moments.

Last but not least, as people change and mature, it's quite common that our interests may evolve. For example, I was involved in one group that focused primarily on marriage and kids. As we have gotten older, we now focus more on our professional goals and our spiritual and physical well-being. As groups and people mature, we should expect the dynamics to shift and be sure to talk about it along the way.

TRUST

As I mentioned earlier, one of my values is trust. I think of trust as a state where our day-to-day actions and what we say align. If we want to build trust, we have to be consistent in how we show up in our relationships. Yes, we might be having a bad day, but how we interact with our Tribes most days should be consistent. We build trust over time through experiences. Trust is earned, and it's a thing of great value to be protected.

However, trust is a provocative success indicator. I have found with females, in particular, sometimes we bestow trust before it's earned. An intriguing study on women, men, and language by Jennifer Coates found that relative to men, when women talk with each other, they tend to focus on people and feelings and reveal more. Females are also naturally more collaborative, wanting to draw out those who are less comfortable talking, while expressing affection and interpersonal concern. Men, on the other hand, are more competitive in their dialogue and avoid self-disclosure, preferring to steer conversations toward more impersonal topics.[32]

I am not suggesting that females only share feelings when they talk or that men never do. I am also not implying that it is wrong to share and reveal personal details. However, as an advocate of creating safe spaces for women to connect, sometimes we need to pause and give the relationship time before we share too much.

To develop deep relationships, we have to connect and communicate in ways that build understanding and develop trust. If we want people to believe us, we have to show up the same, time and time again. Trust is often best earned over time and strengthened by experiences and mutual exchanges. We all benefit when we take the time to get to know each other. Take the time to see if what someone says and how they show up are aligned.

LOVE/GENUINE CARE

At our core, we all want to love and be loved, and so it was no surprise that love and genuine caring featured as a contributor to Tribe success. Love, by definition, is strong affection for one another.[33] The thing is, our feelings of affection and the intensity of our emotions change over time. Feelings are an emotional state or reaction.[34] If you have ever been married or in a relationship, you may have experienced fluctuations in feelings—from madly in love to spitting mad! Love can be a roller coaster.

For relationships to work, I believe we have to shift our thinking to love as a principle. A principle is a comprehensive and fundamental law, doctrine, or assumption.[35] Principles anchor us, guide us, and help to steer us back. I propose that if we stop thinking about love as a feeling or strong attraction, and move toward thinking about love as a principle, our relationships will be stronger.

One of the best descriptions I have seen of love as a principle is found in the Holy Scriptures (1 Corinthians 13:4–8 NIV).

Love is patient, love is kind. It does not envy, it does not boast, it is not proud.

It does not dishonor others, it is not self-seeking, it is not easily angered, it keeps no record of wrongs.

Love does not delight in evil but rejoices with the truth.

It always protects, always trusts, always hopes, always perseveres.

Love never fails.

Now whether you ascribe to the Scriptures or not, to expand the definition of love from more than a mere feeling to this more principled view is potentially a much more effective way to flourish in our relationships. As you interact with your Tribes, try to move beyond the emotion and simply FLOW.

While FLOW can be the natural rhythm of things, it's also a great way for us to remember this concept of love and genuine care as a principle. When faced with conflict, we can choose to react harshly or fall into a pattern of negative thinking. Alternatively, we can choose to leverage our Tribe mindset and remember this simple acronym of FLOW.

When we choose to embrace the principle of love, ultimately we do win. We win in our thinking and in our relationships.

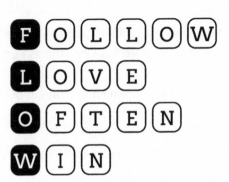

PERSONALITIES

When I talk to most women, they will cite personality as one of the top reasons relationships succeed or fail. We often think it's the personalities of the members that make our relationships successful.

However, I don't believe it's simply personalities that contribute to relationship success. Yes, personalities matter; however, I propose it's more about the degree to which we have personality maturity that matters. When we know ourselves and seek to love and put others first, it's not our personality driving relational success; it's our self-awareness and maturity of our personality. I believe we are who we are, but we can, through reflection and practice, become more flexible, versatile, mature, and principled about how we approach and deal with each other. When all parties routinely consider how we can adjust or be flexible in a situation to achieve a better outcome for all of us, we thrive in our relationships.

I have found that in relationships, there are all kinds of characters with different personality traits. With maturation, we can disagree lovingly and respectfully so as not to create divides. While personalities do matter, there's no perfect mix that make relationships work. At the end of the day, it comes down to how mature and principled we are that matters.

HOW TO THRIVE WITH YOUR TRIBE

Now that we have a deeper understanding of the four drivers of Tribe success, the next question is, how do we thrive with our Tribes? Sometimes when we are busy, we struggle to come up with ways to keep our relationships healthy. I have found that we can have a lot of fun with our Tribes because the list of ways to be creative is endless. Here are a few principles that can help our relationships. I am sure there are others, but here are my top five:

1. LAUGH OFTEN

Life can get overwhelming. When we connect with people we trust, we may run the risk of focusing on the heavy topics. While it's important to find a safe place to deal with issues, for our Tribes to thrive, we have to find time to laugh. Laughing will give life, lighten the mood, and reduce stress.

2. INVEST THE TIME

To build a healthy relationship, set aside time. In my group Tribe, we agreed to meet a minimum of once a month. At times we wanted more, but we tried to keep the cadence realistic so most of us could attend. Years of consistency and time investment have netted beautiful friendships. A Tribe's rhythm can be whatever we want. However, it can also benefit from consistency and taking time to get to know each other. It's time that teaches us about each other and forms the basis of trust.

You need one-to-one time in larger groups as well. Now, this one is a little counterintuitive. If the idea is to get together as a group, why would we need to spend time together one-on-one? In my experience, getting to know individual members on a deeper personal level strengthens the group. In the case of my group Tribe, since we only got together once a month, we assigned "get-to-know-you partners." It was through this process I genuinely gained sisters.

You might be thinking, "I don't have time for groups and one-on-ones!" I know how you feel. We assigned the one-on-one pairings a year at a time to reduce the pain. One-on-one activities were as simple as a phone call or a text, grabbing a tea, or my personal favorite: walking. The net result: our deeper individual friendships created a stronger group.

3. TRIBE STARTS AT HOME

No matter the construct, our Tribes take up time, so it's essential to get our families on board. I know I am guilty of organizing get-togethers, sometimes at the expense of my family. As a result, sometimes I have to rebalance my priorities and remember that my family is my most essential Tribe.

When our families are happy and functioning well, we can be free to thrive with our Tribes. It's also important to note that if our families are the source of our distress and not functioning in a healthy way, we may need the help of our Tribes or even professional support to navigate our family challenges.

4. SUPPORT EACH OTHER IN CRITICAL TIMES OF NEED

Life is hectic. It's easy to get mired down in the pressures of our lives. Some days we need our Tribes to survive. In one of my group Tribes, we have a secret word. Whenever someone says the word, we assemble no matter where we are in the world within a matter of hours, if not minutes. I can't tell you how amazing it is to have not one, but a group of women who will turn on a dime for me when I need them. When our Tribemates need us, they should let us know so that we can do our best to show up.

5. EXAMINE PATTERNS OF BEHAVIOR

We can thrive in our Tribes if we choose to look at the patterns of behavior versus the one-off mistakes that our Tribemates may make. What is the pattern of how someone shows up in our lives, in our Tribes? Have they been kind, supportive, honest, and trustworthy? Or have they been difficult, spiteful, bossy, or hurtful?

In relationships, we should expect people to mess up. When we are faced with something that hurts us or gets under our skin, we can ask, how has this person shown up in my life? With this mindset, we can choose if we want to let the situation go or talk about it and look for a way to move forward. How people have shown up in our lives is one of the greatest tools that we have to assess a relationship.

REMEMBER

When we focus on common interests, trust, love, and personality, we can experience success in our relationships. We have to be intentional about investing in our relationships so they can thrive.

REFLECT

- Examine your five closest one-on-one relationships or the groups you have been a part of. Did they exhibit the four indicators of Tribe success?

- Common Interests: In each relationship, do you share common interests? What are they? How have the common interests impacted your relationship positively? Negatively?
- Trust: Examine these same relationships as they pertain to trust. Do you trust the individuals/group? Do you believe they trust you? If not, why not? What can you do to build a stronger level of trust between you and them?
- Love/Genuine Care: In these same relationships, is your relationship of love/care for them a feeling or a principle? Do you want to deepen your love or care relationship, and if so, how might you do so?
- Personality: Consider your level of personal maturity. Are you a take-me-as-I-am person, or do you try to be flexible when interacting with others? Do you need to make some changes to be more flexible in your relationships?

BE DIFFERENT

- Consider the drivers of Tribe success and ways to thrive with your Tribe. What changes do you need to make to show up differently in your relationships and thrive?
- If you are forming a new relationship, discuss some of the things people enjoy or need for the relationship to thrive.

CHAPTER 14

THE DARK SIDE OF TRIBE

Relationships can be fun, exhilarating, and life-changing. However, there are very few things in life that are good for us that come without some kind of work or effort, and relationships are no different. To illustrate some of the complexities, consider my female group research. According to the data, 38 percent of females have participated in a group that has fallen apart. Here are the top five reasons, in order of prevalence, of why female groups fall apart:

1. Life stage change
2. Distance
3. Personalities
4. Disagreements within the group
5. Other (death, leader change, etc.)

When we choose relationships, we can experience joy. On the flip side, relationships can be complex and emotionally challenging. People shift and change; they love us, leave us, confuse us, and inflict pain. However, the reality remains: we still need connection. The question then becomes, how do we navigate the more challenging aspects of our relationships?

I have talked to enough women to appreciate that for most of us, we want to believe we are above the "petty" emotions that come along with navigating relationships. We push issues to the side or may even look down on those who want to have the real conversations needed to keep relationships healthy. The reality is our emotions, good or bad, need to lead us to take action.

We have discussed life stage Tribes (chapter 8) and personalities (chapter 13). In this chapter, let's explore distance and ten common issues I have either personally experienced or discussed with women while writing this book. Do any of them sound familiar? Reflecting on each one of these issues will help us better prepare to navigate the dark side and thrive with our Tribes.

DISTANCE

When we invest in building a strong Tribe, the idea of leaving or starting over can be exciting, daunting, and depressing all at the same time. The key to navigating the changes that can take place in our lives due to distance is to realize that the goal is not to replace what we had, but rather to create something new.

To explain my point, Susan has lived in at least three different states. In each place, she was there long enough to lay down roots; she was happy, and she loved her Tribes. When I caught up with her a year ago, she was struggling with her last move, which was a few years earlier, and she still had not "found her Tribe." We talked about the concepts in this book, and when we parted, she said she was going to ponder the question: start over, invest virtually, or some other option?

Fast-forward a year later; we checked in, and she shared that the year had not been easy, but she felt at peace. She had taken three core steps to navigate distance and loss of her Tribes:

1. **Be open to new relationships**: During the period following our chat, she had made an effort to stay open and, in the process realized she had always been open. Her mindset of openness and belief in her value constantly reminded her that if a new relationship did not work out, she would be okay. She remained open and kept trying to find her Tribe.

2. **Invest virtually**: While she was searching for her Tribe, to tackle her feelings of loneliness and separation, Susan set social media aside and used that time to intentionally text or have a conversation with her old Tribe(s) virtually. While not as satisfying as a girls' night out, those meaningful quality conversations help to fill some of the loneliness she felt.

3. **Accept the new relationships and value them**: In her new town, people had established relationships, and for years she felt on the outside, unable to find her way in. However, when she shifted her mindset and moved away from trying to re-create what she had to enjoying the time that people could give her, she started to feel more fulfilled.

When we last caught up, she had met two women, and they were in the process of building a formal Tribe. Her final words of wisdom: "Leah, the biggest lesson I have learned is, I can't have one group that supplies everything that I need. It's okay to have multiple Tribes in different places that help me find my own wholeness. I just had to shift my mindset."

Losing our Tribes to distance can be incredibly painful. However, if we believe that we need connections to live our best and healthiest lives, we have to dig deep and make an effort. Effort could mean being intentional about maintaining relationships virtually, or it could mean starting over and enjoying or valuing our new Tribe for what it is. The key is to stay open to the possibilities.

TEN COMMON ISSUES OF TRIBE
1. DIFFERING RELATIONSHIP EXPECTATIONS

Sometimes, people enter into relationships wanting different things. For example, Deana meets Joyce at her local community center and discovers they have several mutual connections. Deana enjoys Joyce's company and is satisfied to connect with her at the center. However, Joyce is in the process of finding her Tribe and wants to spend more time with Deana. Joyce calls, texts, and invites Deana out often. Unfortunately, Deana does not have capacity for the level of relationship that Joyce wants. In order to protect the connection that they do have, Deana needs to be honest with Joyce as soon as possible and in a kind and thoughtful way.

TIP: Take the time to clarify relationship expectations.

2. PROTECTING CONFIDENCE

As humans, we naturally tend to want to share information with others. For example, Ana got engaged and, in a rush of excitement, called her Tribe to share the news, but forgot to tell them to keep the news confidential. Her fiancé's family still did not know. Before she could put the phone down, two members of the Tribe in their excitement posted congrats on Facebook. Sometimes our desire to share is positively motivated, but on occasions and perhaps too often, we share information that is negative or not for us to share. While writing this chapter, I was on Facebook, and a friend posted this quote: "Most people run in packs because they don't feel safe alone. I run alone because I don't feel safe in packs" (author unknown).

I immediately wanted to write back and argue against the sentiment. However, the reality is that sometimes we don't always create safe places for people. When there's a juicy tidbit, we're tempted to tell a spouse or friend and break a confidence.

TIP: Try to shift orientation from a need to "tell," to a need to "protect." It's not always easy, but with practice, we can get there.

3. SPENDING MONEY

In my experience, money can have a meaningful impact on relationships. I have found in one-on-one and group relationships, money, or lack thereof, can deeply complicate things. For example, there could be a situation where Janet wants to travel, eat out, and go to concerts, and it's merely not in Bri's budget.

Or perhaps there are group get-togethers, and one person consistently does not carry a fair share. To complicate matters further, because money is so sensitive, we don't always know why a person behaves one way or another. It could be because they don't have the resources, or frankly, it could be they are cheap and miserly.

When dealing with relationships and money, we have to be mindful and thoughtful about the impact different views or access to financial resources can have on relationships. I was once told a story about a group of friends who went to a restaurant. Most of the friends expected to simply split the bill, while a few wanted individual bills. To the horror of some and the humor of others, they sat in the restaurant for an extra hour while every single person's bill was painstakingly calculated. Another group I spoke to wanted to chip in when people did not have the financial resources. Sometimes that works, but when we can't guarantee we can repeat it for everyone, we can run into complications.

TIP: When engaging on issues of money, make sure everyone is clear about the financial parameters up front to avoid surprises. Don't start anything we might not want to repeat!

4. AVOIDING NECESSARY CONVERSATIONS™

There is a philosophy around having important conversations that I love. I first experienced the approach in a Necessary Conversations™ leadership development program authored by Ann Dorgan, CEO of Gumball Enterprises.[36] When I spoke to Ann, she described the program and philosophy as follows:

"Necessary Conversations™ is based on the philosophy and neuroscience that when we approach fundamentally needed conversations as difficult, dangerous, or risky, we stimulate the fight-or-flight hormone cortisol, which immediately requires us to focus on how we will be managing our fear as we conduct our conversations. So rather than conjuring up fear with these more inward-facing, fear-based words, we reorient ourselves to an outwardly and altruistic focus on conducting the conversations that are necessary for moving our business, our friendships, and our families forward. Most conversations need not be difficult, dangerous, or risky, but rather when orientated externally to the love or care that we have for the other, our business or our families, our conversations become simply Necessary Conversations. In a nutshell, when we engage in conversations with the right mindset, we experience different outcomes."

For most of us, we want to keep the peace in relationships, and we delay addressing issues that bother us. On the one hand, that is healthy. Every little thought that comes to mind does not require us to bring it to the attention of the other person(s). It could be that it's our issue to resolve within ourselves.

At other times we want to take the road of least resistance and say nothing when the most comfortable and fastest path is to address issues quickly when they arise. I was once talking to a friend who hates conflict, and she said, "Leah, I don't want to talk about it. I just want to keep the peace."

I looked at her and said, "Are you protecting the peace or perpetuating the problem?" When we put off discussing the issues that need addressing, those issues may fester and become bigger than they really are.

TIP: Try to talk through an issue as soon as possible after it happens. If it's difficult to move forward, create a deadline to have the conversation. Communicating swiftly and honestly is always the best course of action!

5. SAYING "I'M SORRY" AS SOON AS POSSIBLE

Now that we have developed self-awareness, this one is quite simple: if you do something wrong, say, "I'm sorry," and say sorry quickly. We all have egos, and sometimes we let moments go instead of addressing them quickly.

Haley had a terrible night. Her son was up sick all night with the flu. She felt like she was going to drop down ill at any second. Exhausted, she decides to run to the pharmacy to pick up some medication for her son. She runs into her neighbor Zoey, who starts in with her usual cheerful good morning and, without a breath, proceeds to share a random story. Haley abruptly cuts Zoey off and says, "I can't talk today," while rushing away. This left a surprised Zoey to wonder what happened and if she did something wrong. As soon as Haley started to walk down the aisle, she realized what she did and quickly walked back to Zoey and apologized. Sometimes, there are big things, but more often, it's the little things that come up that create tension.

TIP: When we say or do something to inflict hurt or pain, a quick and sincere apology will go a long way to helping maintain positive relationships.

6. FINDING TIME TO CONNECT

Whether it's a group or one-on-one relationship, as humans, we have different views about how to prioritize time for relationships. Janet has a flexible work schedule and lives alone. She often calls her friend Anna to chat. Anna, on the other hand, has a growing business, two young kids, and struggles to find time to talk to Janet like they used to. Instead of Janet talking to Anna about how to find time to connect that works for both of them, she calls Anna up and tells her she is a horrible friend.

In groups, finding time to meet can be difficult as well. I remember talking to one group that not only struggled to find time to connect but also believed favoritism drove attendance. If the event was held in honor of person A, everyone would show up, but if it was for person B, attendance was sparse. The end result was frustration and some members feeling like they were not valued.

TIP: If we want a relationship to work or increase in depth, we have to put in the time—there's no way around it. Last but not least, try to be intentional about finding time, and in groups, be sure to value people in the same manner.

7. SWEATING THE SMALL STUFF

In relationships, there are many things to get in the way that simply don't matter. In my experience, it's something like a canceled appointment, slip of the tongue, or moody moment. A few years ago, a good friend of mine got sick with a potentially terminal illness, and I remember thinking, "I am so glad I have not wasted our time together sweating the little things." Perhaps it's something that comes with age, but life is fragile and can turn on a dime. When it comes to our relationships, let's try to live with no regrets. If the connection was lost tomorrow, would we be able to say we had no regrets?

TIP: When people trip up, talk about it, or let it go. One of the most helpful ways to determine if we can let something go is to look at the pattern of someone's interactions with us. Is this the norm or an exception? The pattern of how people show up in our lives often clarifies the action we need to take.

8. NAVIGATING HORMONES

This is a topic I did not initially intend to include on the list. However, after connecting with women from all walks of life, it became clear the hormone issue is real! From puberty through childbirth, perimenopause to menopause, and beyond, our bodies are on a roller coaster. Now I don't want to use hor-mones as a catch-all for all bad or strange behavior, but we all have days where we start doing things we don't understand. Perhaps we ate ten chocolates when we intended to eat none. We cried when we planned to laugh, or the thing that would generally roll off our backs turned into an exploding volcano. Somedays, we have moments when we are not ourselves, and our relationships get caught in the crosshairs.

One year, I was struggling with some hormonal issues related to perimenopause. At the same time, I decided to take a trip with friends and took sick while on the cruise. Let's just say the combination of the hormonal issues and the illness while on vacation wasn't my finest moment. I was either bristly or quiet during the trip as I struggled to navigate the changes my body was going through. Before the vacation ended, I said sorry to the group. I was not my usual self, and they kindly understood.

TIP: Hormonal reactions are a real thing as women navigate the stages of life. As soon as we recognize we are out of sorts, it's essential to communicate. Let's pay particular attention to people who were unlucky enough to step into our path while we were in "our moment."

9. HAVING FOMO (FEAR OF MISSING OUT)

One of the most painful issues I stumbled across is women with friends who make them feel guilty about other Tribes. I spoke to one woman who was part of a group for years. She also had one-on-one friends who often made her feel guilty when she spent time with the group. One friend even went so far as asking when she was going to give the group up.

Another dynamic that was excruciatingly painful for the woman was when her friends or acquaintances intentionally and pro-actively tore down the group.

To make this scenario clearer, here is a real example. Danielle is a part of a group. She had a friend Tanya, who wants to be part of the group, but the group is not accepting new members. What Tanya needs to do is to find her own Tribe or let Danielle know she wants to spend more time with her. Instead, Tanya speaks negatively about the group, and Danielle finds out. As a result, Danielle feels hurt and betrayed. Danielle and Tanya's relationship starts to disintegrate.

TIP: If we have a friend who has a Tribe, don't tear it down. We can ask for more time or use the tools in this book to help find and build our own Tribe. When we can celebrate each other for healthy relationships, we are more likely to find and thrive with our Tribes.

10. IDENTIFYING NEGOTIABLE AND NONNEGOTIABLE VALUES

One of the most beautiful things we can do is to look to include people in our lives who are different from us. However, when the values of a person are in stark contrast to our own, the relationship may prove to be complicated. We might need to walk away. Values can be a very tricky measuring stick because it would be rare for someone's values to line up word for word with our own. The key to navigating relationships based on values is to understand the type of value that is in play and what it means for the relationship:

- The first kind of values are **negotiable values**. Negotiable values are defined as values that do not have to align with our own. However, negotiable values bring an added layer of complexity to the relationship, which we have to navigate proactively. For example, I have a friend who was raised with the value of work hard, play later. She struggles with people who don't work at the same pace or stop to take breaks along the way. As a result, she has to regularly remind herself to be careful not to judge her relationships harshly based on her values.

- The second kind of values are **nonnegotiable values.** Nonnegotiable values are values that, if they do not align with our own, make the potential for a relationship (or depth of the relationship) not possible. For example, let's say trust is a strong personal value, and we have a relationship with someone who is a gossip or very judgmental of others. In this case, we might need to walk away from the relationship. Alternatively, we might choose to keep the relationship, but it would be wise not to divulge too much personal information because of misaligned values.

TIP: Let's spend some time thinking about our values and which ones are negotiable and nonnegotiable in relationships. With negotiable values, how might we need to adjust our expectations with people who do not share the same values?

HOW TO NAVIGATE THE ISSUES OF TRIBE

This list of challenges is not intended to be all-inclusive. However, it does capture many of the themes women encounter. So, in addition to the tips we just read, how do we navigate the dark side of relationships in our conversations? To help you, you can leverage this simple conversation strategy that was inspired by the philosophy of Necessary Conversations™.

We can successfully navigate relationship challenges when we LIFT each other up. One of the tools I use to navigate relationship challenges is the LIFT conversation outline. When using this conversation outline, first spend some time self-reflecting on the relationship and the issue. Then when both parties are ready, discuss the situation using the outline together.

LIFT

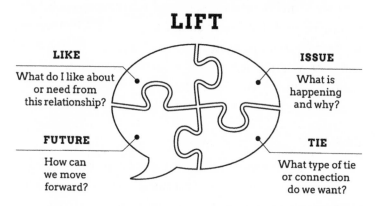

LIKE
What do I like about or need from this relationship?

ISSUE
What is happening and why?

FUTURE
How can we move forward?

TIE
What type of tie or connection do we want?

- **Like:** Why does this relationship exist? What do we like or love about it? What support have we provided to each other in the past? Has our relationship been a good one?
- **Issue:** What is happening? Is this situation normal or an exception? What could each of us have done differently? Could there be outside issues or influences getting in the way (e.g., illness, family, etc.)? Is there another perspective other than my own? How do we feel as a result of what happened?
- **Future:** To move forward, what would it take to forgive? What actions might we need to take to regain trust?
- **Ties:** When all is said and done, what type of connection or tie do we want? Will we be close friends, friends, or acquaintances?

Think about it. If we all made a concerted effort to LIFT our relationships, we would be happier and more fulfilled. The beauty is, the faster we can work through relational issues, the quicker we can clear our mind to think about other things and enjoy life.

REMEMBER

It's natural and normal to experience relationship challenges, and there are some issues unique to women. When we are intentional about navigating the challenges of relationships and LIFT them through our actions and conversations, we can live our best lives with our Tribes.

REFLECT

- Go back and review the list of relationship challenges. Are there any particular issues that surface in your relationships more often than others? What tips can you use to navigate the challenges?
- Think about a current relationship challenge or a time when an issue repeated over and over in your mind. How can you or could you have used LIFT to think through issues and navigate to a quick resolution?

BE DIFFERENT

- If there's a live relationship issue you are working through, give yourself a time deadline, use the LIFT conversation outline, and proactively resolve the issue.
- If you have a one-on-one or group relationship where relationship depth is a goal, get together and talk through the challenges listed in this chapter. What are the views and opinions of each person? Agree on a few strategies to help LIFT your relationship when issues arise.

CHAPTER 15

BACK FROM THE BRINK

Now that we have explored what it takes to create and navigate the complexity of relationships, we have to answer the following question: When a relationship ends or breaks, what is our path back from that place? The place where we hurt someone, or they have hurt us.

According to my group research, 27 percent of female groups who break up are able to recover. The reasons they are able to rebuild include love, common interest, personal commitment/ investment in the relationship, and redefining the group's purpose. The reasons we persist in our relationships are deeply personal and varied. However, when they break, practically there are two paths: the Path of No Return or the Hard Trek Back. Let's explore them both.

THE PATH OF NO RETURN

Sometimes when our relationships break or suffer, there's no going back. The damage is done, and we have to deal with the loss. Having experienced it myself and in talking to others, it's almost like suffering through the death of a loved one. The question is, how do we recognize when a relationship is on the path of no return?

In my case, I had a friend, and to this day, I am not sure what caused her to walk away. One day she was fully engaged, then I started to notice she was saying no to invitations and slowly pulling away. Weeks turned into months, and she was absent more and more. I tried to figure out what was going on, but she kept pulling away. One day she stopped connecting. For a while, I fought it, but in the end and without explanation, she had moved on and started a new life. I heard rumors about why, but I never got an answer from her. To be honest, I was devastated. This was a person I had spent hours with, dreamed with, and here I was at the end with no explanation.

As I look back, the signs were clear: a proactive, intentional pulling away with no reason. In speaking with others, sometimes it's less ambiguous; the person simply tells us the relationship is over, walks away, and no longer communicates. When we find ourselves on the path of no return, I think there are three helpful strategies to employ.

COMMUNICATE OUR RELATIONSHIP PREFERENCE HUMBLY AND CLEARLY

When we feel a relationship ending, it's critically important that we are honest with the other person about what we are thinking and feeling. For example, I was talking to a woman who said that her friend was pulling away. I asked, "How do you feel? What do you want from the relationship?"

She shared her raw feelings with me: "I really care about our friendship and I miss her."

I asked, "Have you told your friend, using that exact language?"

You guessed it: she had not. When the people we care about start to pull away, this is the time to be humbly transparent about how we feel. If we miss them, tell them; if we love them, let them know. This is not the time to get stuck in our feelings and let relationships splinter.

On another occasion, I had a friend who started to pull away due to some severe personal challenges, which she did not share with me at the time. When I saw it happening, I was very clear about where I stood with her. I called her up and said, "I just want you to know, I value our friendship—in fact, more than value. I love you and want the best for you. I hope that includes our friendship. However, I will respect your space if you choose to move on."

When someone is down the path of no return, they may not answer or tell us they are done. In this second situation, thankfully, my friend asked me to be patient as she worked through her issues, and eventually, our relationship returned to normal. It is important to be clear and leave nothing on the table so that if you find yourself at the end of the path of no return, you will have no regrets.

EXPERIENCE THE STAGES OF GRIEF

When we lose a relationship, we often go through the stages of grief: denial, anger, bargaining, depression, and acceptance. Each of us navigates these stages differently. Some stages we go through more quickly than others, and some we experience simultaneously. As we navigate our grief, we will feel deeply. It is in these moments that we should be kind to ourselves and be thoughtful about the other person. In the long run, we will find more peace if we take this high road. This is not the time to berate ourselves or trash the other person everywhere we go. The goal is to find acceptance and get to the other side as whole as possible.

LEAN ON OUR TRIBES

Sometimes, it's hard to let relationships go. However, when someone decides to no longer be a part of our lives, we have to work toward a place of acceptance. We may find, though, that when we are in the midst of pain, we forget there are other people who love us and support us. The pain of that one loss can overshadow all of the belonging we have. It's crucial during these times to lean into our support networks to help us rebound and move on. We can find trusted friends or counselors to help us navigate the loss. If we don't have belonging outside of one relationship, it may be time to regroup and start over. Starting over is a harder path, but use the tools in this book to help find belonging.

To this day, I have not meaningfully reconnected with my friend who chose to walk away. I am okay. In fact, she is okay, too. The key is to navigate grief and then leverage the belief about our value and belonging to move forward. There are so many people in this world who need us, need our connection, gifts, and talents. As hard as it is to accept, sometimes the path of no return is an open door to new possibilities.

THE HARD TREK BACK

There is a second scenario to explore when our relationships break. What happens when someone has hurt us or perhaps we have hurt them? Some days we want to do the work, and other days it's extremely difficult.

I remember one situation where I had to make the trek back. I was in a difficult personal and professional place. With a punishing work schedule and two small kids, I was utterly over-whelmed by life. As a result, I began to pull away from a friend who was a really great supporter over the years. She had not changed. However, I was full, with no extra time, and I needed space. I am not particularly proud of how I showed up at that moment, but it was a part of my growth.

Now to know her is to love her. She is a genuine people person who will bend over backward and give you the shirt off her back or the food off her plate. It started in small but subtle ways. I called less. I invited her over a little less. I needed to create space. The space turned into a vast river, which eventually nei-ther of us could figure out how to cross. Sometimes when we are going through our stuff, we need a fresh perspective and/or a space to get our heads on right. It's in these moments we may push the people who mean the most to us away. It's critically important to recognize these moments so we can either pull people close or simply say: "I need space right now."

What's important to note is that while I wanted more space, I still made an effort to keep our families connected. Even though I was in a different space, I knew that it would have been incredibly selfish for me to cut off the relationships for everyone. Time passed, and while we were not as close, we remained friendly. Thankfully my friend was patient with me.

Eventually, knowing that I had to fix what I had broken, I invited her on a girls' trip. We talked for hours and were deeply honest.

In the end, I realized we were experiencing a relationship shift or change.

My mom once gave me some great advice. My parents have been married for nearly fifty years, and my mom often says, "In marriage, couples shift or change every five years or so." The person we were five years ago is not the same person we are today.

I believe those shifts happen in our nonmarital relationships as well. Sometimes life or circumstances force us to grow or change. When those shifts happen, we have to be careful that our relationships don't suffer in our growth processes. In my case, my career and parental responsibilities were pushing me to change how I allocated my time and how much emotional capacity I had to invest in my nonfamilial relationships.

When relationships break, sometimes they are never the same, and that is the new state. In other instances, with humble, thoughtful conversation and a recommitment to openness, we can find a more transparent place for the relationship. Today between my friend and I, when things surface, we hit it on the head right away. If I am retreating, she will tell me. If she is acting inconsistently, I will call her on it, too. While not perfect, it's actually a much more comfortable relationship than it was twenty years ago.

Is the trek back easy? No. Some days, it's difficult to forget the pain of the past, particularly if the person hurt us or we hurt them.

Can it be done? Yes. The rebuilding process requires work. Getting back to a place where our intentions and our behaviors align takes time and does not happen overnight. It takes two people making a decision to make the relationship work. When we are in the midst of it, we might be tempted to be belligerent and say, "I don't want to put this kind of effort into a relationship that's not even my spouse!"

Again, maybe it's age and sense of mortality, but I often ask myself: Do I want to live the rest of my life disconnected from this person? If I did completely disconnect, would I have regrets? If my answers are no and yes, respectively, I have to put myself out there and be prepared to do the work to get the relationship back on track.

In summary, here are the key points to remember as you make the hard trek back:

- Recognize that everyone, including you, changes over time.
- Be honest with yourself and the other person about your investment capacity (time, effort, emotion).
- Be very careful not to break the relationships of others when you are going through a shift.
- Talk it out. Ideally, talk through whatever "it" is so that the other person understands where you are on your journey.

REMEMBER

When relationships start to go sideways, communicate how you feel clearly and quickly. If necessary, accept the loss and lean on your Tribe to move on. If the opportunity presents itself, do the hard work to restore trust.

REFLECT

- Have you ever lost a relationship? Think back. Is there anything you could have done differently to preserve it? How might you have communicated more effectively? Were you humble enough to communicate how important the relationship was to you?
- If you have a relationship you are mending, are there any conversations you need to have that can help to rebuild trust?

BE DIFFERENT

Life will naturally cause you to grow and change. Every six to twelve months, take time to reflect on the shifts happening in your life. List them and examine who you need to communicate these shifts to in order to preserve your relationship. How will and when will you communicate these shifts?

CHAPTER 16

PAIN PRODUCES GROWTH

A TRIBE STORY

 My name is Elise. I have messed up and been hurt. I have learned, laughed, found a new Tribe, and I am better for it. This is my *Assemble the Tribe* story.

As a child growing up, I did not have sisters. I was close with my brothers, but there were certain things I couldn't share with them. I observed my mom, and every time she got together with her sisters, there was a lot of laughter. As a result, I grew up knowing the positive attributes of female relationships.

I begged my parents for a sister, but it never happened, so I looked for close relationships within my parents' Tribe. I developed very close friendships with five other girls who were around the same age as me. We talked about everything and did everything together. It was a great childhood, and over time the sting of being the only girl eased as I connected more deeply with my "sister" Tribe. We sang together and we defended each other; we were inseparable.

I did not know it at the time, but there was a divide lurking within our friendship that would raise its ugly head in the years ahead. Often when we get comfortable and relax with groups and friends, our behavior is either at our best or sometimes at our worst. I know for my part, I was not as sensitive to the feelings of one group member, something I would later regret with my whole being.

The six of us were always together. There were best-friend relationships and one-on-one, close bonds within the six, but for the most part, we always spent time together. We knew we would grow old and raise our kids together. However, life would not be kind to us in that way, as I moved to Bermuda to follow my heart, leaving my sister-friends behind. As the years passed by, we continued to connect, for special occasions and girls' weekend trips, but it was never quite the same as when we lived in the same town.

One year, we finally managed to get back together to celebrate a milestone event. Little did I know it would change the course of my life. As the event kicked off, I was excited. The five people I loved most in the world were with me. As is often the case with groups, sometimes, some days, personalities get in the way. When I stepped away from the group for a few minutes, words were said. Those words, said to my friend by another member of the group, ripped through her heart like a jagged knife on fire. Not wanting to ruin the special moment, no one said a word; and I, none the wiser, went on with life, happy we had spent the time together.

A few weeks later, I decided to call my friend to find out how she was doing and bask in the memory of our get-together. Unfortunately, she was not in, and I didn't think anything of it. The following day I tried calling again, and the phone rang with no answer. A week later, I called back, and there was no answer. A month later, I reached out again. Then all of a sudden I realized that every single time I called, she was either not there or not available. Something didn't seem right.

I tried again and again for several months. Nothing. Then one day, I got a long email from her. The section I remember the most read:

"For our entire lives, you have always put the feelings of others above mine. The incident at our reunion was another painful reminder that that has not changed after all these years. The incident was a deep source of pain. As a result, I have decided that we can no longer continue as friends."

As I was reading, my life flashed by, and I could clearly see the times when the two of us were scheduled to do something, and at the last minute, someone would call, and I would cancel. For years I believed my friend was relaxed about everything. I knew deep down in my heart she wouldn't mind. However, as I digested the fact that it had bothered her for years and she never told me, a new realization set in. It was very painful reading the message, and initially, when I read it, I thought, *No, our friendship is not over. I don't accept it.*

I wrote back, "I would rather we talk and try to work things out."

She immediately responded, "I'd rather we go our separate ways."

In all honesty, it was one of the hardest breakups I have endured. It was tough, worse than what we see in the movies. Not wanting to give up, I fought for our friendship by trying to open the lines of communication. However, as the years went by, I realized she had indeed moved on. I held on to the hope that the relationship would heal. Still, after years of trying, she eventually sent me a short, but tactful note suggesting it was time for me to move on.

I was devastated, and in a moment of tears, I remember another dear friend putting her hands on my face and saying, "Elise, you have to let this go. You no longer have a friendship."

"If she cannot talk to you by now, you have to let it go."

At that moment, something clicked. I accepted it was over. When I talk or think about it now, I can get through it without crying because it is what it is. I know there's no going back. That final realization was painful. It was almost like going through the stages of grief, and now for me, there was finally resolution.

Today, there are times when the remaining five of us get together, and my heart is still sad. I wish she was still here, but I know it just can't be.

As with all things in life, experience either breaks us or teaches us lessons to make us stronger. The loss of my friend caused a change in my mindset about relationships. I feel that no matter how close we are with someone, we should not take the friendship for granted. Sometimes we feel as if, because we are so close, we should be able to do or say anything and our friends will always understand.

Even when we are close with someone, we still have to take their feelings and opinions into account. Had I realized how insensitive I was when I was younger, I would have moved heaven and earth to change my behavior because that is the kind of love I had—no, have—for her. When I start relationships now, and I have found several new Tribemates, I am a much more thoughtful and sensitive person.

In summary, are relationships tough? Yes! However, our lives are so much richer when we have them.

Do I still love my friend? Yes!

Am I still sad some days about the loss of friendship? Yes!

Am I a better, more sensitive person? Yes!

I have learned that throughout it all, I am still okay because sometimes our greatest pain produces our greatest growth, and so for that, I am grateful.

Here are my Top Five Ways to Be Different:

1. **Don't Take Feelings for Granted**: Ask for feedback. When we open the door for our Tribe to be honest with us and we are honest with them, it can make the relationship(s) stronger.
2. **Be Intentional**: Communicate feelings, whether positive or negative. Talk things out. If a relationship is important, communication is not optional.
3. **Don't Be Afraid**: Don't let past relationship pains keep you from bringing new people into your circle; they can add value to your life. Give others a chance.
4. **Know When to Move On**: When someone tells you there is no friendship or relationship, or it is beyond repair, accept

their truth and move on. But don't close yourself off to new relationships; stay open.

5. **Accept That Relationships Are Complicated**: Relationships might be complicated, but there is nothing better than finding the right mix. Keep searching until you find your Tribe.

PART 4

Be Different (Beyond the Tribe)

CHAPTER 17

THIS ONE'S FOR THE GIRLS

WE ARE STUCK

This chapter is for moms, grandmothers, aunts, godmothers, dads, uncles, and mentors who are helping to bring up the next generation of young ladies. As we have learned throughout this book, navigating relationships is complex. In today's society, navigating relationships and friendships as a young girl or teen without years of experience is a challenge. Add technology and constant social media access on top, and you will find the most complex younger generation in the history of the world.

Did you ever have a negative experience as a young girl? Have you sat by and watched a child or adolescent girl struggle with the pain of rejection? How old were you? How old was the girl? According to my research:

- 63 percent of women were a member of a female group at some point in their lives.
- 71 percent of women had negative experiences in female groups.
- 50 percent of those negative experiences happened while

the women were under the age of 18, 25 percent under the age of 13.

- 54 percent of all women never saw positive female group relationships as children.

Essentially what the data is saying is that during our adolescent and teenage years, when our brains are rebooting, hormones are raging, and bodies are changing rapidly, these are the moments when many of us experienced our most painful moments of rejection. As a result, our trust and sense of belonging is challenged.

In my experience, most women didn't know how to handle lack of acceptance in their young, formative years. It was hurtful, and therefore the pattern continues to get passed on to the next generation due to a lack of knowing how to address these situations. When I started to see the pattern repeat in my daughter's life, initially, I was stuck, too. The narrative I have heard for years and years is that girls are just mean and catty. There's nothing that anyone can do about it.

During one difficult season, I watched my daughter and several of my friends each experience the loss of an important friendship at the same time. With my front-row seat to their pain, I knew that the challenges of relationship were not age-specific and they were not going away. It was time to tackle it head-on.

THE GOOD NEWS

Since my mom gave me that personality test at the age of eight, I have been on my own journey to build stronger, healthier relationships for myself and others. I continue to make mistakes and learn. It has not always been easy, but it has been worth it.

However, as I watched my daughter and friends struggle, with increasing urgency, I knew it was time to do it differently. I wanted my daughter's experience or at least her ability to navigate through relationship challenges to be different than mine.

According to the data, 81 percent of women believe in giving back to future generations. We want to make a difference for them. Additionally, when we as children observed positive female group relationships, we were more likely to want the same for ourselves. When I dug into the data a bit further and asked, "Where do we observe these positive relationships as children?" the top three answers were:

1. Mothers and friends
2. Family (aunts, grandmothers, etc.)
3. Organizations (churches, clubs, etc.)

Our girls are watching us! If that's the case, the way we show up as adults in our relationships has a tremendous opportunity to impact future generations. The question we have to answer is, what can we do to help future generations bypass the relationship challenges that many of us have lived?

TO SPEAK IT YOU HAVE TO LIVE IT

I believe to truly understand a situation, and develop a solution, sometimes we have to live it. Little did I know the opportunity for me to do just that was about to appear on my doorstep.

I was traveling several time zones away when I received a call from my mom: "Your daughter had an awful fight with her friends and cried herself to sleep last night."

Immediately I was transported back to junior high, and my heart broke for her. I quickly shifted into how-do-I-solve-this mode.

My first thought was, "I have to call my daughter and talk this out!" However, it was late at night in Bermuda, so I had to wait until the next evening when she returned home from school. When we finally spoke, though, she was elusive and didn't want to talk about the situation. It was a difficult moment of restraint for me. Part of me wanted to press her and drive for resolution. However, my gut instincts said that I needed to respect her boundaries and give her time to process what was happening.

Given that my mom was there and actively engaged as her support system, I decided not to press further. Instead, I told my daughter that I loved her, she was special, and we would find a way to navigate through the situation together.

When I eventually arrived home, the conversation was the same, "I don't want to talk about it, Mom."

Two weeks stretched into a month, a month into six weeks, six weeks into eight. With each passing day, I watched my generally vivacious daughter shrink into a fog of sadness. Not sure how to help, I did the best I could. I kept asking how her day was, made her favorite foods, tucked myself next to her, and watched a few good movies. However, while her mood seemed to lighten in the moment, she would revert to a rather sullen child, put her earphones in, and go to her quiet place.

As a parent, I was of two minds. First, was this normal "relationship" stuff? Or was this deeper? Did I need to do more? According to the World Health Organization, an estimated 10–20 percent of adolescents globally experience mental health conditions, which remain underdiagnosed and undertreated.[37] Globally, depression is the fourth leading cause of illness and disability among adolescents ages fifteen to nineteen years old. My challenge was figuring out, is this nothing, or is it a big thing? What should I do?

I decided to put my sleuthing hat on and do some digging. I needed a window into what was going on. Thankfully, some of the information landed in my lap when parents sent me snippets of the chat. With a more comprehensive view, I sat back to take it all in. I was dismayed at how mean and unkind the girls were, and frankly, I was surprised at my daughter as well. I found myself asking, "Who is this child?"

What's fascinating about what I discovered is that the root of the issue—at least the part of the story that involved just my daughter and her friend—came down to personalities and communication. We discussed the impact of personalities in adults in chapter 14, so it's not surprising that kids struggle with the same issues.

My daughter lives out loud and is very expressive, while her friend is more reserved. The result was a natural clash of styles as the girls struggled to figure out how to communicate with each other effectively. To complicate matters, with this generation most conversations occur over text instead of in person, which created a big mess! After weeks of sitting on the sidelines watching the train head toward—and then fall off—the cliff, I knew it was time to act.

TWO PARENTAL MINDSET TRAPS

This eight-plus-week saga crystalized three dangerous traps that we can fall into as parents if we are not careful:

AS LONG AS MY CHILD IS NOT AFFECTED, I'M GOOD

Up to this point, I was pleased with my parental journey. My kids had no major relationship issues. My son and daughter were well adjusted. I knew there were issues around them, but as long as they were not touched, I was okay. I learned that, as parents, as we become aware of issues happening around our kids, we have to engage. If the problems are happening around them, the likelihood is high that, at some point, it will touch them. Of all of the mindset traps I found, this one is the hardest. How do you go outside of your comfort zone and try to navigate the complexities of relationships with parents you don't know and who likely have strong views of their own? I mean, who wants to put themselves out there in that way? Frankly, I hated the idea, but I started to make the rounds with the parents to see if they saw what I was seeing. It was uncomfortable, but what I discovered is that most of the moms felt the same way—at a loss!

I KNOW MY CHILD—SHE WOULD NEVER

The reality is that during puberty, we don't know our kids at all, and they don't even know themselves. According to new neuroscience research, there's a fundamental reorganization of the brain taking place in adolescence. During this time, environmental influences exert particularly strong effects and sometimes harmful impacts on our kids.[38] As a result of these changes, the child we knew last year is not the child we know today.

With each day of adolescence, the child is growing and becoming more independent. However, in many ways, they are still quite fragile, which means, as parents, on some days, we are mostly back at square one! Thankfully I found the research before my daughter's saga started, so I was at least more informed about the neurological and physiological changes. As a result, I believe I was more patient than I might have been. I knew that in this season I would not understand her as well as I thought I did. Frankly, with her changing brain and body, some days, neither would she!

SLAY IT OR THEY MIGHT HAVE TO KILL IT

I once heard a great speaker say something to the effect of, "If we don't murder our bad habits now, our children and possibly our children's children will have to kill them."

This quote weighed heavily on me as I navigated the situation with my daughter. I mean, we can't protect our children from every negative situation, and frankly, sometimes they need to go through them to grow. However, as a parent, what was my role? What was I to do? In navigating the issue to a conclusion, I identified five actions we can take as caring, concerned adults to impact future generations.

1. SHIFT MINDSETS

As the data proves, how we conduct ourselves in our relationships with other women matters. When our kids see us talking positively about other women, maintaining healthy relationships, it matters. Language matters as well; for example, let's not tell our girls all women are mean and catty.

As girls and women, we are layered, complex, and in the case of adolescents, changing individuals. As we shift our mindsets and our language, we can tackle the real-life issues and challenges that our girls face more constructively.

When educating our girls about navigating relationships, we can also teach them the Tribe-building formula:

Believe + Belong = Be Different

Often, when relationships turn sideways because we are in pain, we tend to forget about the value and the belonging that we already have. Before these times of distress, we can teach our girls to lean into their value and belonging to navigate the challenges. If your child has no belonging, as a parent, you may want to consider how to help them find a Tribe to belong to. I encourage my daughter to remember the formula when she is in conflict. When I asked her how the formula helps her, she blew me away with her answer:

"The formula teaches me that even though fighting with a friend can be sad and upsetting, I still have people who care about me, so it's not the end of the world."

She continued, "Instead of getting depressed and upset, I should focus on my other friendships and try to fix the situation if I can. When I focus on my other friends, it makes difficult situations easier to deal with."

"I also learned that sometimes, when you are going through a difficult friendship issue, if you can fix it, it can even make the relationship stronger."

2. GET EDUCATED

Nearly one in three adolescents will meet the criteria for an anxiety disorder by the age of eighteen. Further, adolescent girls are more than twice as likely to experience depression than boys.[39]

According to Staci Danford, a gratitude neuroscientist, "This is the first generation of youth who are growing up in a purely global society. In the absence of technology, for our generation, it was easier to know where we belonged—at school, at church, with family friends. In today's global world, young people are developing connections and comparing themselves to everyone, and anxiety and depression have skyrocketed. As a result, the belonging this generation experiences is not close or physical. The steady barrage of comparison pushes them to a place where they feel like they don't belong."

As parents, it's critical to take some time to learn more about what is happening to our children during adolescence, both physically and neurologically. Having an enlightened view makes us more understanding and will benefit our children for years to come. In addition to educating ourselves about what's happening with our children, we have to build our own relationship and conflict management skills. We can't help our children navigate their relationship challenges when we have not taken the time to build those skills in ourselves.

As parents, once we understand the changes our children are going through, we have to engage. Ask questions; go on dates to talk randomly. If you have more than one child, make sure to find time to interact one-on-one in addition to family time.

3. HELP YOUR CHILD EXPAND THEIR TRIBE

Kids need dedicated time and space to deepen relationships. Consider how we deepen our relationships as adults. Our relationships form over coffee, during trips, on long walks, or by working together, just to name a few. It's incredible that we miraculously expect our kids will develop and deepen relationships at school when 80–90 percent of their time is dedicated to schoolwork.

As parents, we can create spaces for our kids to build relationships. My husband and I are always open to allowing our kids and their friends to hang out at our home. I have also found that I learn a great deal when I shuttle them around in the car! If your child has a few close friends, help them to leverage that belonging and expand their friend-circle. Trust me, they will likely not do it on their own. In doing so, you can help them understand the importance of broad friend circles and relationships. If one relationship breaks, it won't break them.

4. FIND A MENTOR

Last but not least, we can help our children expand their Tribes by helping them to find a mentor. I know the relationship that I had with Alexa at the age of fourteen was life-changing for me. If you can spare the time, be that person for someone else's child. Sometimes all it takes is a quick text or catch-up, where you are genuinely present to let them know you care.

I spoke to one young woman whom I mentored in her tween and teen years, and she said,

"Having a mentor definitely made a difference in my life. It was great having someone who was older to look up to. I think having you in my life at such a young age gave me a sense of stability, and I felt heard. Knowing that I had someone other than my immediate family who was always there mattered. I think that was really important for me at that age and continues to be today."

5. TAP INTO YOUR TRIBE

You might think: "Good for you, Leah. But I work three jobs, and I don't have time to do all of that." The reality is, some days we just can't do it all. That is why being open and expanding our Tribes does matter. On occasion, our Tribes can step in and help when we are unable to do so. Over the years, my husband and I have made an intentional effort to build our family Tribe. Today, when we need a parent break or one of our friends needs a helping hand, we step in and help each other. When we deepen our relationships, particularly with the parents of our children's Tribes, we can support each other when we need it most.

As we wrap up this chapter, let me finish the story about my daughter and her friend. I called the other mom, and we talked it over for a few hours. We agreed that even if the friendship changed, it was important that the relationship survived to the point where the girls could interact amicably. We decided to facilitate a conflict resolution conversation. To help prepare, each girl completed a questionnaire. The questions encouraged them to explore the friendship using the LIFT model. If needed, go back to chapter 14 and pull out the specific questions to help shape a conversation.

LIFT

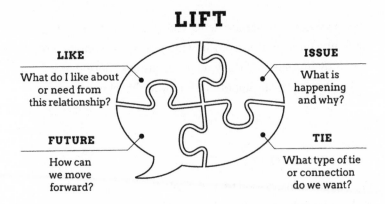

LIKE
What do I like about or need from this relationship?

ISSUE
What is happening and why?

FUTURE
How can we move forward?

TIE
What type of tie or connection do we want?

After each girl had had the opportunity to think about the questions, we took them out for snacks. I am proud to say that we did not facilitate, but rather sat across the room from them as they, like two mini-adults, worked it out.

The outcome: a decision that the friendship was important, and over time they would work to help build it back. The girls agreed to talk directly to each other, not over text, when feelings started to get in the way. For the two girls, I believe this was a life-changing, growing moment. For me, it was a connection with a mom on a new level. I also had a tear-jerking moment when my young lady came to find me, gave me a big hug, and said, "Thank you! Thank you, Mom, for helping me work it out with my friend. I could not have done it without you!"

On the off-chance you are thinking, "This is great, but my daughter is already in crisis!"

As parents, we can't protect our kids from the pain of relationships. However, we can love them, support them, and hopefully help them find at least one strong bond, and then continue to build their Tribes. There was a study that was published in the *British Journal of Psychology*. The research found that having one bond, one quality relationship, had a tremendous impact on the resilience of kids versus kids with lower-quality relationships.[40]

In my experience, it is beneficial to help your child find that one quality relationship. However, it is also important to help them expand their Tribe, too. This is important because one day, the crisis could be with that best friend! During that crisis, support might mean reminding them that they belong in more than one place, or it could mean helping them to start over. Even as adults, there's no easy way to deal with the loss of a relationship. When our kids are in pain, sometimes the only thing we can do is to provide loving support, and if needed, get professional help. The hope is that with belonging and help, in time, they will find their way.

As I think about the future, my story is still not complete. I am still living and navigating the challenges of raising two teens. However, I believe that as we continue to educate ourselves and become more open in our thinking, we pave the way for the next generation to experience Tribes differently. It's going to be hard work, but that is something worth fighting for!

REMEMBER

Our children are the most connected, complicated, lonely generation in the history of the world. As parents, we need to stay engaged and acknowledge that we can't do it all. We can shift our mindset and tap into our Tribes to help us raise the next generation and do it differently.

REFLECT

- Have you had or watched someone else have a negative

experience with a female or female group as a child? How has that experience influenced how you think about female relationships today?

- How can you use the information in this book and chapter to support the young girls or even boys in your life?

BE DIFFERENT

- Take the time to educate yourself on what is happening to your child at the various stages of development.
- Commit to getting to know your children's Tribes. Get to know them better. Consider adding the parents of the kids to your Tribe.
- Help your child think about who they might want as a mentor, and proactively support the development of the relationship.
- Bonus: Find a child to mentor and give back. It's in the giving that we sometimes are genuinely changed!

CHAPTER 18

IMPACT YOUR WORLD

When we are happy and thriving in our lives with our Tribes, it's easy to think we have arrived. What more could we want in life? However, what if that state of living was in some ways, just the beginning?

WHAT'S MY PURPOSE?

For many of us, purpose is a nebulous, almost unobtainable state that we continue to search for and often eludes us. We attend conferences, read books, and build vision boards in hopes that our purpose will spontaneously crystallize. We pray and hope that at some point, we will know for sure, no fooling, that it's the thing that we were created to do.

Purpose, by definition, is the reason why something is done or the reason why someone or something exists.

What if I told you that you didn't have to search for purpose? Would you believe me?

The reality is most of us are searching for something that is right in front of us. In fact, it is inside of us. Our true purpose lies at the intersection of our design (who we were created to be) and our desire to share it with others.

Think about it: if our purpose is the reason we exist, then our purpose is not something to search for. By definition, purpose has to be something that already exists inside of us. Every life that we touch allows us to live out our purpose. Living in true purpose means we take who we are—our gifts, strengths, talents—and we proactively look for opportunities to share them with others.

One of the women who has had an incredible impact on the world is Oprah Winfrey. I remember sitting on my couch as a child watching her show with my mom. Oprah was like no one I had seen before. She was a mix of humor and realness that made me feel like I was sitting in her living room.

By reading her story or following her career, we know she was born to a single mother. Oprah grew up with her grandmother in Mississippi for the first six years of her life. While her grandmother was strict, Oprah said her grandmother gave her the foundation for her success. Even as a child, Oprah knew she was special and that she was different.

During an interview, she once said, "I remember standing on my back porch and my grandmother was boiling clothes and I was watching her from the back porch. I was four years old and I remember thinking, 'My life won't be like this; it will be better.' And it wasn't from a place of arrogance; it was just a place of knowing that things could be different for me somehow." At the age of three, she started to recite pieces at church, and the church members would tell her grandmother she was gifted.

Even though she didn't know what it meant, she just started to believe it.[41]

Oprah's belief in herself, combined with her natural gifts and talents, propelled her from a little-known newscaster to the host of one of the highest-rated talk shows in Chicago. Today she is known as the "Queen of All Media" and one of the most influential women in the world.

As we think about and consider her story, it's not a purpose or future that was handed to her, but a purpose that was innately part of who she was. In her OWN master class in 2011, Oprah said, "This is what I know. It does not matter where you come from; what matters is now, this moment and your willingness to see this moment for what it is, forgive the past, take responsibility, and move forward."[42]

I have come to understand, from the top of my head to the soles of my feet, that the core of who we were created to be is something we already have. It's not something we have to search for, find, have handed to us—we already have it. That said, it's not always easy living a life of purpose. When we are shifting and moving into a more purpose-lived experience, it's uncomfortable. We are pushing ourselves, stretching ourselves into areas where we may have never ventured before. To truly live it, we have to choose to shift our mindset and believe we are capable of more. With hard work and leaning into the best of who we are, we can do more, be more, and give more.

MY PURPOSE AND MY TRIBE

"I got it, Leah, but what does this have to do with my Tribe? Our Tribes are not responsible for helping us live our purpose."

Correct! It's not our Tribe's responsibility to help us live a purpose-filled life. However, if we are living in our purpose, have Tribes who support us, affirm us, push us, and catch us when we fall, how much more likely are we to thrive and do great things?

Having a Tribe, the right Tribe, is life-changing and empowering. When I think of all of the times my Tribe pushed and supported me, it brings tears to my eyes. For example, the support I had while writing this book was priceless. On days when I had a block, or I felt like it was just too big to pull off and make it happen, someone would call, "How are you doing? I know the book is going to be great, and I can't wait to read it. I need your book. The world needs your book."

Those few words reminded me that my work mattered and pushed me to pick myself up and dig deep. Because if that person whom I loved needed my book, then I had to deliver.

It's not the role of our Tribes to define our purpose, but when we live into our purpose, our Tribes will naturally push us, support us, and help us to grow.

PURPOSE AND IMPACT

Some readers might be thinking, "Okay, but my life is so full. I have work, family, all these relationships, I can't fathom how I could ever do more."

When we consider the idea of a more significant impact, sometimes we get stuck on our capacity to do more. For many years I thought that if it was my idea, it was mine to carry alone, and I simply did not have time. However, I have found most people, most women, want to have an impact. In my group research, 64 percent of women believe groups should try to give back and make an impact. Also, 53 percent of women have found ways to do so. Most of us think of impact as a vast project or movement. However, impact can be as simple as a kind word or hello.

Once I was having a conversation with one of my group Tribes, and we were discussing what we would do if we could live our dream lives. What struck me about that conversation is that most of the things people dreamed of doing were not shallow, but were more altruistic. When talking about their dreams, almost every single person wanted to give back and make a difference. One person wanted to provide high-quality meals to people who did not have regular access to nutritious food.

As we sat there, I asked, "Why do we have to wait until it becomes our dream job? Is there something we can do today?" Right there and then, we started to plan how to make it happen.

Sometimes impact is a movement that takes on a life of its own, and sometimes it's about creating a small or simple moment that makes an impact. When we get out of our own way, we will find we don't have to chase impact, but rather the opportunities for impact are everywhere. With a little effort and the support of our Tribes, we can make a difference.

STORIES OF IMPACT

When I started *Pay It Forward Bermuda*, my goal was to impact lives, to let people know that even if the world around them was falling, in that moment, they mattered. As a solo act, I was able to surprise people and pay for their groceries, pay a bill, or some small thing. However, it wasn't until I leveraged the power of the Tribe that the real magic happened.

I called a few members of my Tribe (male and female) over to the house and shared my vision of a day when we would blanket our entire island with acts of kindness. The excitement was palpable, everyone in the group wanted in, and we got to planning. We partnered with a few companies, and then each person decided what their personal random act of kindness would be. People purchased gifts, made homemade baked goods or crafts; whatever they were able to do, they found a way to give. Through various unsolicited donations, we were able to purchase vouchers for groceries and medicines. We also partnered with coffee shops and gas stations to give away free coffee and newspapers. We worked hard to prepare, and the night before the excitement was palpable—it was like Christmas had arrived.

The following day we started at 6:00 a.m. During the next twelve hours, fifty volunteers performed more than 2,500 random acts of kindness in one day. The video, testimonials, and moments of personal impact were some of the most rewarding of our lives. This one day was a remarkable example of how leveraging our Tribes can exponentially increase our impact.

As we close out this chapter together, it's a great opportunity to take a step back and consider: What's inside of me? What are my gifts, strengths, and talents? How can I use them in little ways, and in BIG ways? What story do I want my life to tell? I am created for more.

REMEMBER

Our lives become more precious, more meaningful, when we give the best of who we are to others. When we take our belief in our value and leverage the belonging and power of our Tribes, that is when each of us, in our own special way, can truly change the world.

REFLECT

- Pull out your list of three to five gifts, talents, and strengths from chapter 5, and if you want, add a few more. Take a piece of paper and write each of your gifts, talents, or strengths in a list on the left side of the page. On the right side of the paper, make a note of the degree to which you use the gift or talent. Use the following scale: I use this gift, strength, or talent: all the time, some of the time, or not at all. See example below.

	I use this gift, talent, or strength...		
Gift, Talent, Strength	All the time	Some of the time	Not at all

- As you review your list, pay specific attention to the gifts, talents, and strengths you use some of the time or not at all. Spend some time thinking about why you are not leveraging them.

BE DIFFERENT

- Review your list of "some of the time" and "not at all" gifts, talents, and strengths, and come up with at least one to three ways that you can use them with more regularity. Write them down and commit to taking action.
- Think of a specific purpose project you have thought and dreamed about. What would it take to get it done? If it's really big, is there a small piece or fraction of your dream that you can start today or test? Think of ways that your Tribe can support you, ask them for their perspective and ideas, and then take a stab at it.

CHAPTER 19

A BLANK PAGE FILLED

A TRIBE STORY

 My name is Mel. Finding a Tribe did not come easy for me. As a young child, I experienced pain and rejection. However, I have learned to think about Tribes differently. By changing my mindset, it has awakened a desire for me to walk in my purpose. It has also made me want more for my daughter and the next generation of girls. This is my Tribe story.

TRAGEDY STRIKES

As a child, I don't remember having much self-awareness. Some people say they loved writing at a certain age, and some people loved playing outdoors, climbing trees, or something specific. I don't recall dreaming about getting married and having kids. I have none of the light bulb moments some people have when they say,

"Oh, I remember ____ as a child."

"My mom always used to say ＿＿."

"My daddy used to say ＿＿."

In my early years, I had no idea life would become this blank page that, at times, I was not coherent enough to fill in. I was born into a stable home with two parents full of happiness and adventure. It was the kind of home where my mom and dad said, "I love you," every single day. We hugged and cuddled. In addition to my parents, I had the best godmother in the world. She was always there—loved me, guided me, took me shopping; you name it. Her relationship with my mother was probably my first observation of what a female bond looked like.

I was content, well adjusted, and happy. However, as fate would have it, at the fragile age of twelve, all of my safety and security was ripped away. One day a preventable accident snatched my mom away and my world changed forever. Without any notice, she was stolen from me, and my world seemed to stand still. While I was not aware at the time, I believe part of me stopped dreaming, any moments of significance forgotten.

MY NEW NORMAL

When tragedy strikes, even though we are still reeling, life never skips a beat. Ready or not, I returned to my day-to-day routine, hoping to find some normalcy. In elementary school, I had a few friends, but there was never a deep bond. There was no bestie, no belonging, just me passing through life.

As a child of mixed race, I was teased mercilessly and often found myself in fights. I never provoked the arguments, but if I needed to defend myself, I did what I had to do.

When I transitioned to middle school, I remember connecting with one or two girls, but they were more acquaintances. Without a deep support system, I needed to focus on something, so I immersed myself in sports. Sports became my friend, my way to tackle the world, and I excelled. Instead of friends to hang out with, it was basketball, softball, track—any kind of sport to occupy my time.

One thing I remember is excellent relationships with female teachers. All through middle school and high school, I clung to women who I thought were influential. Perhaps they represented a mother figure.

I remember during high school, there was one teacher in particular who took the time to invest in me. Ms. Eve was vibrant, full of energy, loved health and fitness, and actually looked a lot like me. She started a club for girls, which I joined. I distinctly remember feeling a sense of belonging. For the first time in my life, I felt like I was home. Today we laugh about it as she reminds me how I followed her around like a little puppy, completely unaware.

From that point forward, Ms. Eve was there through all of the significant transitions and milestones in my life. Perhaps it was the fact that our family life and backgrounds were similar; maybe it was that she loved sports as much as I did. Ms. Eve loved me and treated me like her little sister. She was real, authentic, and I felt it. For the first time in years, I let my guard down and relaxed into the belonging I had found.

As I look back, Ms. Eve and my godmother took the time to invest in me, to love me. Without knowing it, they saved me because everyone needs belonging, and even though they didn't have to, they created a space where I could be loved and feel safe.

MY SEARCH FOR TRIBE

Years later, I went off to college, which I would describe as four years of experience. In hindsight, it would have been an excellent opportunity to be more intentional about finding my Tribe. Instead, I concentrated on one close friend, boyfriends, and classwork to occupy my time. Life didn't leave much time to develop relationships outside of this comfort zone. I don't believe I wanted more or looked for more. I was satisfied.

While I did not recognize it at the time, I was in my own way searching for my Tribe. I joined a sorority, and I formed a bond with my line sisters (the women who joined the sorority with me). We stayed connected over the years through our chat group and celebrated milestone anniversaries. However, outside of those touchpoints, I don't see them much, which makes sense; it was a bond, a connection for that stage of my life.

THE SHIFT

Four years of college sped by. Soon I found myself back at home out in the work world. I was active, busy, but something was missing. The real shift came when I realized, after a series of bad decisions, that life had turned me into someone I did not recognize, and who I knew I wasn't. I started to feel this intense urge to change the trajectory of my life—I needed to shift. I became more aware of the value of Tribe and saw it as a void in my life. I wanted to belong. This awareness made me more proactive. I started to listen to inspirational podcasts and videos. I read self-development books, and the messages inspired me to find connection, something bigger than myself.

It was around this same time that I connected with a friend who was organizing a pilot women's conference. I thought to myself, "I need to be there." I had never been to a women's conference before. In my mind, I pictured what I had seen on TV: big room changes, rows and rows of people, surface-level interactions. Instead, it was an event that I experienced intimately. It was there that I was introduced to the concept: "Behind every successful woman, there is a Tribe of successful women who have her back."

The event was particularly powerful for me because I wasn't feeling valued professionally and was questioning my skills and abilities. The conference reminded me I had value. It was uncanny how accurately the weekend touched the exact areas of my life where I felt like I was drowning. I was also able to connect with positive, like-minded women, several of whom I now consider as part of my Tribe.

The conference changed the trajectory of where my life was heading, personally, professionally, and spiritually. I would not have started my journey without experiencing and learning how to believe in myself. Today, I am more self-aware, I have matured, and I am more settled and more comfortable in my own skin. I am building my Tribe bit by bit. I am finding new relationships as my authentic self with no apologies. I love that.

MY DESIRE AWAKENED

With a renewed sense of who I am and a growing Tribe, a fire started to build inside me. A big part of my journey became about loving myself and leaning into my strengths and passions. Sometimes this scares me. At other times it energizes me. The past three years have taught me I have what it takes to realize my dreams and make a difference. At one point, I even remember saying, "I need to be part of something bigger than myself."

I followed my heart and established what I'm calling a "social enterprise." It's an organization designed to help strengthen, enrich, and celebrate the mother-daughter bond. The mother-daughter relationship can be organic, but it also goes through challenges. I hate when I hear young girls tell their mothers, "I hate you." It's a phase, I realize. However, when I hear those words, having lost my mom early in life, I hurt for them. My deepest desire is to impact the mother-daughter bond and keep it healthy.

Knowledge is power, and through our programs, we help mothers identify critical stages of development. We aim to help equip the mother and daughter with tools to navigate various stages and issues to keep the bond secure.

When I reached out to the moms for our pilot event, most said, "This is just what I need right now. Your timing couldn't be better." I know what I am doing makes a difference.

IMPACTING MY WORLD

The beauty of Tribes is to help us realize our dreams and support us in ways we did not know we needed. Before I kicked off my first event, I reached out to a woman I met at the women's conference. Cara was so inspirational and impressive. I invited her to lunch to talk about my vision. In less than an hour, she helped me clarify my vision and affirmed me for the impact I wanted to make. Sometimes I struggle with feeling unqualified to do or to say certain things. I get stuck because of fear of what people might say. The words of affirmation I received from Cara were confirmation I was on the right track. Right after lunch, I immediately went back to my computer and sketched out my full vision for the program.

Oprah once said, "Find a problem and solve it." I don't think that moms and daughters are a problem per se. However, helping them create stronger relationships is a huge opportunity.

Some days I am still angry. I wish my mom was here, and from time to time, I struggle to forgive her for leaving me so early. However, in spite of my pain, qualifications, background, and experience, I still believe I can make a difference.

As I think back on my story, even with my incredible loss, without realizing it, I have always had a Tribe. Ms. Eve, my godmother, godsister, and a few close friends were my first Tribe. They were there and created belonging when I needed it most. However, I want more. I want a bigger Tribe. I want to create a sense of Tribes for the mothers and daughters who attend my program. I am excited about the possibilities and what this looks like in the future. I have personally experienced how Tribes impact lives, visions, and make a difference. I can't wait to see how my social enterprise evolves and the lives it will touch.

One thing I am most excited about is that no matter my past, in so many ways, I have a clean slate. My life is fresh with new opportunities, not only for me but for my daughter. While I can't give her a Tribe, I can teach her to value herself and be secure in her own skin. I can show her some steps to be a better friend. I can teach her how to find mentors and connect with other women. I am excited about the future. I am more self-aware than I have ever been. I no longer have a blank piece of paper.

Here are my Top Five Ways to Be Different:

1. **Listen:** Before projecting your thoughts and feelings, take the time to listen and consider their sensitivities and the impact your words might have on others.
2. **Affirm:** Take the time to affirm others and yourself! When self-limiting thoughts or words are said, be kind, and forgive yourself and others.
3. **Have Courage:** Have the courage to connect with new women who share your interests and drive. Finding a supportive Tribe can give you the courage to grow and reach your dreams.
4. **Expand:** Expanding your Tribe with new relationships does not mean you don't still love and appreciate former friends. However, you have to make sure you make an effort to tell them and show them you still care.
5. **Be Intentional:** Be intentional about communicating with your Tribe. Support them when they need it.

CHAPTER 20

BELIEVE + BELONG = BE DIFFERENT

MY TRIBE STORY

About midway through writing *Assemble the Tribe*, I needed a getaway, a "Me-cation," to anchor me spiritually and give me space to think. I was struggling with my identity. I left my executive position in an industry I had worked in for nearly twenty years to embark on a career break. I had no plans other than to spend time with my family, write this book, and consider future options. As a consummate planner who is always on the go, I felt a bit lost. So, I booked a bucket-list trip to one of my favorite countries in the world: Italy.

My first day in Italy was intoxicatingly beautiful. As the sun rose, I opened my windows, breathed in the salty air, and gazed at the beautiful waters of the Amalfi Coast. Perched high on a cliff in the distance, I could see the famous city of Positano with boats anchored in the bays below. Nonetheless, I spent ten to twelve hours writing. The words flowed as easy as the springs running down the side of the mountains.

The following day was a bit overcast, but riding high on my writing success, I was determined to head out and explore the surroundings. I jumped into a small water taxi, and as we took off, it began to rain. Immediately, I was annoyed with myself for not taking the umbrella as the hotel staff recommended.

Instead, I took a deep breath and said to myself, "Self, no negative self-talk today," and I turned my face upward to take in the salty breeze and gentle raindrops.

Within minutes we pulled up to a small restaurant recommended by the hotel. It was simple with small wooden beams marking the four corners, shaded by a beige tarp, with a bright red sign announcing the name of the establishment.

What I remember most from that first moment: it was loud and chaotic. Everyone right down to a bouncing baby was eating, laughing, and having a great time. I found what I thought was a patron line. For ten minutes, I stood and watched as local waiters scurried about carrying humongous plates of pasta and seafood.

After about fifteen minutes, everyone was seated except me, even though I was not the last to enter the restaurant. I started to become agitated. Pulling me back into the moment, that small voice in my head said, "Leah, you're in Italy. It's your first day. You have time; just relax."

The maître d' finally came over and I gave him my reservation information. He pivoted and surveyed the restaurant. I had every expectation he was going to stick me in a corner on my own. However, he surprised me, stopped midway inside the restaurant, and sat me next to a stylish mature couple. The wife wore an elegant black, white, and gray cover-up with a sleek black fedora, dark shades, and burgundy lipstick. The husband sat on the other side of the table, looking quite dapper in his white and blue collared shirt paired with blue Bermuda shorts. He topped off his look with a straw fedora and dark shades.

Within moments the woman leaned over and said, "Hi, my name is Di."

I discovered the two were married for fifty-three years. They took turns sharing their marriage secrets. Her secret: take care of your man's needs. Well, she didn't say it quite like that, but that's what we will print. His secret: treat every day like a date—full of love, anticipation, and kindness.

As the minutes ticked by, Di turned the conversation toward me. "What do you do?"

Not really sure how to define my new identity, I said, "I used to be an HR executive. At the moment I am taking a career break to spend time with my family and write a book."

Di asked, "What are you writing about?"

"I am writing a book called *Assemble the Tribe*. It's about how to create and sustain healthy relationships."

As the words came out, I felt they were inadequate. Di leaned toward me and took a long pause, so long my ego started to get wound up. However, once again, a small voice said, "Relax; calm your ego. Quiet your mind and listen."

As she continued to lean toward me, Di quietly said, "Leah, but what if people create relationships based on a values system that is wrong?"

I paused to digest her comment and said, "You know, Di, that's why I'm writing the book. We don't always form relationships in the right way. My book will propose a new values system that brings us closer together."

Almost as if not convinced, the conversation moved on, and I was left pondering how I could articulate the book's message more effectively.

We talked for hours about love, family, and life, but when it was time to leave, they begged me to stay. We took a picture together. I hugged them and said goodbye, not fully appreciating the impact these moments would have on me in the days ahead.

I walked the tiny streets of Positano, snapping pictures as I made my way up the steep hills to the shuttle pickup spot. It was blisteringly hot. I counted the minutes to when the air-conditioned shuttle would arrive and rescue me. At about fifteen minutes after the hour, a blue van pulled up and two couples jumped in. I ran over and asked, "Good Afternoon, what hotel is this shuttle for?"

There was an awkward moment of silence as the driver stared at me. Perhaps it was my accent? Maybe it was something else? Whatever the reason, he refused to answer. My pressure started to rise again as I pulled out the hotel brochure to fan myself.

He glanced down at the brochure and said, "Are you staying at that hotel?"

"Why, yes, I am staying at this hotel."

"Okay, well, hop in." I wanted to be annoyed, when again, the inside voice said, "Just relax. Get in the van."

As I sat down, a woman leaned over to say: "Hi, my name is Lana!"

During the five-minute drive, I learned she was from the United States. A few years prior, Lana and her husband met their companions while traveling through Europe. They enjoyed traveling together, so they planned a bucket-list trip to Italy.

I asked, "How is your journey so far?"

They regaled me with stories of the beauty in Rome and Pompeii. "Last night we met another guest at the hotel who told us Capri and the blue grotto was the highlight of their trip. With such a strong recommendation, we booked a private boat and are headed to Capri on Saturday."

"I am glad to hear Capri is terrific. I am planning to visit on a group tour on Sunday."

Without skipping a beat, Lana said, "Hey, do you want to join us on the boat?"

Wanting to say no, but feeling compelled to say yes, I hedged. "I have a few tours booked, so let me see if I can unravel my plans. If I can, I will go with you."

When we arrived back at the hotel, I fully intended to decline. However, that small voice inside me was insistent, "Go!"

For reasons I cannot figure out to this day, I canceled my other plans and sent Lana a text: "I was able to change my plans! See you on Saturday!"

That evening while relaxing in my room, I needed to work on getting clarity on this book's tagline. I need people to get it within a matter of seconds. I spent hours playing with various iterations and developed a beautiful, ranked spreadsheet of options.

Growing tired and a little frustrated, I asked myself, "Leah, what do you want people to believe and feel when they put down your book?"

"I want people to believe they matter, and they have value. I want people to find belonging. I want everyone to shift their mindset and leverage that belief and value to be different." To me, Be Different means to be:

Open to new relationships

and

Thriving in the relationships we have.

I sat there digesting my thoughts, and the words "Believe, Belong, Be Different," settled clearly in my mind. It was almost perfect!

One thing was wrong. I needed one word that meant: Be Different. It needed to start with a "Be-" like Believe and Belong. For nearly an hour, I looked for a new word, with no success.

The next day I had the courage to try the new language out on my driver. I was pleasantly surprised when immediately he got it. Later that afternoon, I ran into Lana again, and she invited me out to dinner. The conversation with her friend and their husbands was familiar:

"What do you do?"

"Oh, you are a writer?"

"What are you writing about?"

I smiled because this time I had answers. "I am writing a book called *Assemble the Tribe*. The book is about believing in your value, finding belonging, and shifting your mindset to live a different life with your Tribe."

There was a slight pause, and we launched into a lengthy conversation about the state of the world and how we need to be open to thinking differently about our relationships. As we laughed, talked, and ate great food, I sat back in my chair, smiling, knowing in my heart I had unlocked the story I needed to tell.

The next day I was writing my thoughts in my journal before we left to head out to Capri. While writing, my iPhone began to play a song called "Different." The song was about changing who we are, such that our characters are no longer recognizable, but different. As I sat there listening, I was reminded of another song by Will I Am. It's called: "Be Nice." The core words of the song are: "Be Different, Be Nice."

As the lyrics to *Different* flowed over me, I knew I did not need to change the tag line. The words "Be Different" were perfect.

Feeling full and amazed by the specificity of the message, I smiled as I walked down the steep path with my new friends, ready to get on the boat. As soon as we were settled in the boat, our driver delivered bad news, "I am so sorry, we can't go to Capri today. The water is too rough." We were all disappointed, but wanting to enjoy the day, we settled for a sunny boat ride toward the city of Amalfi.

As we traveled the coast taking in the sights, enjoying the sunshine and the seas, I looked at all the boats: small boats, big boats, some without names, some with names written in Italian. As we rounded the last turn into Amalfi, my eyes were drawn to a particular boat because the awnings were green, one of my favorite colors. As we moved closer and closer, it was then that I almost fell overboard in shock, surprise, and then delight. The name of the boat was written in English, the only English I had seen that day. In big bright red letters: Think Different.

The irony is I went to Italy looking for answers. But the clarity these experiences provided was uncanny, surreal, overwhelming, and life-changing. I might have missed all of these encounters and lessons if not for being open to them.

In these moments, when I had chosen to think differently and have a Tribe mindset—to be more open and connect with strangers—my questions were answered. As a result, I was leaving Italy with new friends and clarity on the purpose of this book.

The point of My Tribe Story: No matter what you have believed in the past, each of us has the power to Believe, Belong, and Be Different. We can change our lives and the lives of those around us. All we have to do is be open to shifting our mindset, thinking differently, and choosing to live our best lives by Assembling our Tribes.

IT'S YOUR TURN

Assemble the Tribe is more than a book. It's my life. It's my passion! Even before I knew what a Tribe was or defined a Tribe-building formula, the magnetic power of Tribes pulled at me. For more than twenty years, I have coached colleagues, clients, and friends. I've created movements and events that bring people together. I have lived, changed, and been restored by this formula: Believe + Belong = Be Different.

I know it works because I have seen fears conquered, career trajectories skyrocketed, and personal lives transformed all through the power of Tribe.

Tribe is a journey of mindset. Tribe is not a destination. We will never wake up to find that all aspects of our relationships are perfect. Somedays, we mess up. We allow the negative stories we tell ourselves to take over. We say the wrong things or shrink back from our own potential.

The good news about Tribe mindset is we don't have to be perfect. Just be open.

My challenge is that you don't just read and then close the pages of this book, but load the Tribe mindset software into your life. Examine where you are on **YOUR** Tribe journey:

BELIEVE

Are you exploring the best parts of who you are?

BELONG

Perhaps you are remembering, searching for, or expanding your tribe?

BE DIFFERENT

Maybe you are trying to be more open?

Whether you are exploring one part of the Tribe Mindset formula or all three, your next best step starts with you. Together, let's change the future with our Tribe mindset.

- Living longer, healthier, happier
- Embracing our value and the uniqueness of who we are
- Being open, trustful, flexible, and letting the little things roll off our backs, and speaking life into situations
- Supporting women and raising the next generation of women to do it better than we ever could
- Living into the unique purpose that lies inside each of us

Life is so short. No day is promised to any of us. What are you waiting for? Live each moment like it's your last!

Believe in Your Value.

Because if you are alive, you have value.

Find Belonging.

You need people and they need you.

Be Different.

Be open, kind, loving, thrive.

Tap into your purpose and make an impact!

Remember this formula:

Believe + Belong = Be Different

Internalize it, Explore it, Apply it, Live it!

It's Your Turn!

It's Your Time

to

Assemble Your Tribe!

ABOUT THE AUTHOR

LEAH J M DEAN is a coach, author, speaker, and former chief human resources executive who has worked with leaders throughout the world to build high-performing teams, or tribes, for twenty years. A passionate believer in assembling tribes for greatest impact, Leah is the founder of numerous programs and events designed to help women and girls find their tribes and do great things. Leah lives in Bermuda with her husband and two children. Join the tribe and learn more about Leah's work and tribe mindset philosophy at www.leahjmdean.com.

CONNECT WITH LEAH DEAN ON SOCIAL MEDIA

- Facebook: @leahjmdean
- Instagram: @leahjmdean
- LinkedIn: https://www.linkedin.com/in/leahjmdean/
- Twitter: @leahjmdean

WORK WITH LEAH

EXPERIENCE A SHIFT

LEAH has a simple yet powerful message to share with anyone who wants to live their best life. The secret to changing your life comes down to one powerful yet simple formula:

BELIEVE + BELONG = BE DIFFERENT

To book Leah to speak or work with her, visit www.leahjmdean. com.

NOTES

1   "Tribe," Merriam-Webster (n.d.), in *Merriam-Webster.com dictionary*, retrieved May 7, 2020, from https://www.merriam-webster.com/dictionary/Tribe.

2   M. Fried, *The Notion of Tribe* (Menlo Park, CA: Cummings Publishing Company, 1975).

3   "Group," Merriam-Webster (n.d.), in *Merriam-Webster.com dictionary*. Retrieved March 1, 2020, from: https://www.merriam-webster.com/dictionary/group.

4   Mike Woolridge, *"Mandela Death: How he survived 27 years in prison,"* BBC News, December 11, 2013, retrieved August 22, 2019 from: https://www.bbc.co.uk/news/world-africa-23618727.

5   Larisa Epatko, "How Mandela Survived His Years in Isolated South African Jail," *PBS New Hour*, July 18, 2013, retrieved August 22, 2019, from https://www.pbs.org/newshour/world/nelson-mandela-1.

6   Debra Umberson and Jennifer Karas Montez, "Social Relationships and Health: A Flashpoint for a Health Policy," *Sage Journals*, October 8, 2010, retrieved August 22, 2019, from https://doi.org/10.1177/0022146510383501.

7   Julianne Holt-Lunstad, Timothy B. Smith, Mark Baker, Tyler Harris, and David Stephenson, "Loneliness and Social Isolation as Risk Factors for Mortality: A Meta-Analytic Review," *Sage Journals*, March 11, 2015, retrieved August 22, 2019, from https://journals.sagepub.com/doi/10.1177/1745691614568352.

8   Meira Epplein, Ying Zheng, Wei Zheng, Zhi Chen, Kai Gu, David Penson, Wei Lu, and Xiao-Ou Shu, "Quality of Life after Breast Cancer Diagnosis & Survival," *Journal of Clinical Oncology*, February 1, 2011, retrieved February 11, 2020 from https://www.ncbi.nlm.nih.gov/pmc/articles/PMC3058286/pdf/zlj406.pdf.

9   Candyce H. Kroenke, Yvonne L. Michael, Elizabeth M. Poole, Marilyn L. Kwan, Sarah
     Nechuta, Eric Leas, Bette J. Caan, John Pierce, Xiao-Ou Shu, Ying Zheng, and Wendy Y.
     Chen, "Post Diagnosis Social Networks and Breast Cancer Mortality in the After Breast
     Cancer Pooling Project," *ACS Journals*, December 12, 2016, retrieved February 11, 2020,
     from https://acsjournals.onlinelibrary.wiley.com/doi/epdf/10.1002/cncr.30440.

10   Society for Personality and Social Psychology, "Health Determined by Social
     Relationships at Work," ScienceDaily, October 3, 2016, retrieved August 21, 2019, from
     www.sciencedaily.com/releases/2016/10/161003214129.htm.

11   Debra Umberson and Jennifer Karas Montez, "Social Relationships and Health: A
     Flashpoint for a Health Policy," *Sage Journals*, October 8, 2010, retrieved August 22,
     2019, from https://doi.org/10.1177/0022146510383501.

12   Ibid.

13   Society for Personality and Social Psychology, "Health Determined by Social
     Relationships at Work," ScienceDaily, October 3, 2016, retrieved August 21, 2019, from
     www.sciencedaily.com/releases/2016/10/161003214129.htm.

14   William J. Chopik, "Associations among Relational Values, Support, Health, and Well-
     being across the Adult Lifespan," *Wiley Online Library*, April 19, 2017, retrieved August
     22, 2019, from https://onlinelibrary.wiley.com/doi/abs/10.1111/pere.12187.

15   "Great Women Rulers," *Women in World History*, 1996–2003, retrieved January 20, 2020,
     from http://www.womeninworldhistory.com/rulers.htm.

16   Jess Huang, Alexis Krivkovich, Irina Starikova, Lareina Yee, and Delia Zanoschi,
     "Women in the Work Place 2019," *McKinsey*, retrieved January 21, 2020, from https://
     www.mckinsey.com/featured-insights/gender-equality/women-in-the-workplace-2019.

17   University of Montreal, "Women Outperform Men When Identifying Emotions,"
     ScienceDaily, October 21, 2009, retrieved January 29, 2020, from www.sciencedaily.com/
     releases/2009/10/091021125133.htm.

18   TM Wizemann and ML Pardue, eds., *Exploring the Biological Contributions to Human
     Health: Does Sex Matter?*, Institute of Medicine (US) Committee on Understanding the
     Biology of Sex and Gender Differences (Washington, DC): National Academies Press,
     2001), retrieved May 4, 2020, from https://www.ncbi.nlm.nih.gov/books/NBK222288/
     doi: 10.17226/10028.

19   Shelley E. Taylor, Laura Cousino Klein, Brian P. Lewis, Tara L. Gruenewald, Regan A. R.
     Gurung, John A. Updegraff, "Biobehavioral Responses to Stress in Females: Tend-and-
     Befriend, Not Fight-or-Flight," *Psychological Review*, August 2000, retrieved August 29,
     2019, from https://psycnet.apa.org/doiLanding?doi=10.1037%2F0033-295X.107.3.411.

20   Brian Uzzi, "Research: Men and Women Need Different Kinds of Networks to Succeed,"
     Harvard Business Review, February 25, 2019, retrieved August 29, 2019, from https://hbr.
     org/2019/02/research-men-and-women-need-different-kinds-of-networks-to-succeed.

21 Bryan Kolb, Robbin Gibb, and Terry Robinson, "Brain Plasticity and Behavior," *Psychological Science*, 1995, ebook June 17, 2013, retrieved January 20, 2020, from https://www.psychologicalscience.org/journals/cd/12_1/kolb.cfm.

22 Steven J. Spencer, Claude M.Steele, Diane M.Quinn, "Stereotype Threat and Women's Math Performance," *Journal of Experimental Social Psychology*, January 1999, retrieved January 13, 2020, from https://doi.org/10.1006/jesp.1998.1373.

23 "Population, Female (% of Total Population)," The World Bank, retrieved January 20, 2020, from https://data.worldbank.org/indicator/SP.POP.TOTL.FE.ZS.

24 Amy Morin, "7 Scientifically Proven Benefits of Gratitude That Will Motivate You to Give Thanks Year-Round," *Forbes*, November 23, 2014, retrieved January 13, 2020, from https://www.forbes.com/sites/amymorin/2014/11/23/7-scientifically-proven-benefits-of-gratitude-that-will-motivate-you-to-give-thanks-year-round/#2f0ae638183c.

25 "U.S. Adults Have Few Friends—and They're Mostly Alike, *Barna*, October 23, 2018, retrieved September 18, 2019, from https://www.barna.com/research/friends-loneliness/.

26 Ibid.

27 Ibid.

28 Christien Ro, "Dunbar's Number: Why We Can Only Maintain 150 Relationships," *BBC*, October 9, 2019, retrieved on December 30, 2019, from https://www.bbc.com/future/article/20191001-dunbars-number-why-we-can-only-maintain-150-relationships.

29 "Relationship," Merriam-Webster (n.d.), in *Merriam-Webster.com dictionary*, retrieved March 1, 2020, from https://www.merriam-webster.com/dictionary/relationship.

30 Lisa Fritscher, "Phobias: The Psychology Behind Fear," medically reviewed by Steven Gans, MD, *Verywell Mind*, November 7, 2019, retrieved February 25, 2020 from https://www.verywellmind.com/the-psychology-of-fear-2671696.

31 Lisa Fritscher, "Phobias: The Psychology Behind Fear," medically reviewed by Steven Gans, MD, *Verywell Mind*, November 7, 2019, retrieved February 25, 2020 from https://www.verywellmind.com/the-psychology-of-fear-2671696.

32 Jennifer Coates, *Men, Women, and Language*, Third Edition (London & New York: Routledge Taylor and Francis Group, 2013).

33 "Love," Merriam-Webster (n.d.), in *Merriam-Webster.com dictionary*, retrieved May 27, 2020, from https://www.merriam-webster.com/dictionary/love.

34 "Feeling," Merriam-Webster (n.d.), in *Merriam-Webster.com dictionary*, retrieved May 27, 2020, from https://www.merriam-webster.com/dictionary/feeling.

35 "Principle," Merriam-Webster (n.d.), in *Merriam-Webster.com dictionary*, retrieved May 27, 2020, from https://www.merriam-webster.com/dictionary/principle.

36 Reference is to the Necessary Conversations™ leadership development curriculum authored and owned by the leadership development company, Gumball Enterprises, located in Seattle, WA, USA.

37 World Health Organization, "Adolescent Mental Health," October 23, 2019, retrieved February 25, 2020, from https://www.who.int/news-room/fact-sheets/detail/ adolescent-mental-health.

38 Kerstin Konrad, Christine Firk, and Peter J Uhlhaas, "Brain Development during Adolescence Neuroscientific Insights into This Developmental Period," Deutsches Arzteblatt International, June 2013, retrieved on February 25, 2020, from https://www. ncbi.nlm.nih.gov/pmc/articles/PMC3705203/.

39 Kathleen Ries Merikangas, Jian-Ping He, Marcy Burstein, Sonja A Swanson, Shelli Avenevoli, Lihong Cui, Corina Benjet, Katholiki Georgiades, Joel Swendsen, "Lifetime Prevalence of Mental Disorders in U.S. Adolescents: Results from the National Comorbidity Survey Replication—Adolescent Supplement (NCS-A)," Journal of the American Academy of Child and Adolescent Psychiatry, October 2010, retrieved on January 14, 2020, from https://www.ncbi.nlm.nih.gov/pubmed/20855043.

40 Rebecca Graber, Rhiannon Turner, Anna Madill, "Best Friends and Better Coping: Facilitating Psychological Resilience through Boys' and Girls' Closest Friendships," British Journal of Psychology, June 25, 2015, retrieved March 1, 2020, from https://doi. org/10.1111/bjop.12135.

41 "Oprah Winfrey 1991," American Academy of Achievement, August 24, 2018, retrieved January 6, 2020, from https://www.youtube.com/watch?v=PEZIjUA6u_U&feature=youtu.be.

42 "Oprah on Taking Responsibility for Your Life | Oprah's Lifeclass," Oprah Winfrey Network, October 21, 2011, retrieved on January 6, 2020, from https://www.youtube. com/watch?v=Dp_cmLfJZ1w.